The Forced March
from Vietnam to Kentucky

By

Patrick J. Fitch

RoseDog Books

PITTSBURGH, PENNSYLVANIA 15238

RoseDog Books
585 Alpha Drive
Suite 103
Pittsburgh, PA 15238
Visit our website at www.rosedogbookstore.com

ISBN: 978-1-4809-7049-6
eISBN: 978-1-4809-7073-1

"Everybody's your friend when you're rich, famous or dead!"

Charles Eugene Fitch, my father, observing the mourners at the funeral of his own father, Eugene Charles, during the viewing of the body at Beinhaurer's Funeral Home, Dormont, Pa 1956

"I am none of the above!"

Patrick
Winter, 2016

Antecedent

Publishers rarely draft a work of any writer unless he or she clearly defines the intended audience. Mine is the journey shared with my peers born post World War II. The end of the World War II and the saga of the atomic age shattered the illusion of peace. The tension of the Cold War ushered the advent of us Baby Boomers. The fall of the Berlin Wall then ushered the birth of the alleged Millenials, the postscript to Generation X. Hopefully the vignettes herein will provide some insight from Woodstock to Facebook and now the horror of Islamic-fascism, the cult and business of death. The anecdotes described articulate a lifetime honed by combat, college and a high school teaching career. Teaching: Also sometimes borderline combat!

And, yes, I love elliptical sentences.

This is the précis of that prescient, asymmetrical journey and a de facto peripatetic autobiography. Each essay is almost a "stand alone." I just reach into the pillbox of a cluttered mind and focus on the target at hand ranging from the serious to the banal. Kind of like an artillery strike!

Like most writers, all I just wanted to do was just that....write. The world of the mundane, trumped by the need for groceries, rent, a series of mortgages, marriage and attendant children stifled this pursuit. I left the local newspaper business for more money. After all, journalists are "revenue depleters," not "revenue generators" unless you have the breakthrough of a Tom Clancy or Lee Child. The business of publications depends on income and that is the purview of the sales staff, not those who create the content. It isn't anyone's insidious design. It's just the caustic reality of publication "life." Writers are the "raison d'etre" but they don't pay the overhead.

The death of my father at 15 jolted me into an adult world for which I was woefully unprepared. Then to be tossed out of undergraduate school was the second trauma. It was something about that 1.6 GPA! Beer, testosterone and estrogen in abundance are often a toxic triple team for a 19-year old. I plead guilty on all counts. Expulsion in August; Parris Island in October. It was a short three-months span from naïve to "recruit." My forced march may seem random. It's not. Many others share and traversed it. We all trace the road of life said with very different road maps and GPS. My guiding bromide, first uttered by a former Catholic Marist priest, Berrien H. Zettler, begins my daily routine: "The past is infallibly true!" It was true when he said it to a Novitiate audience of potential Catholic priests with the Society of Mary (Marists) in 1964 at Rhinebeck, NY and remains so today. Writer and audience all have a past and a present. Past is history. Present is challenge. Focus is future. Keep the future vision in the "V-Ring" and slough onward. Persistence and patience are the precursor catalysts to success.

And finally: I welcome any and all feedback on what follows, either positively or negatively. Contact me at patfitch@vic.net.

I'm easy to find and don't hide. You will get a response!

And, finally, special thanks and affection to Jose R. Santana and William B. "Bosco" McElhaney whose inspiration and support helped bring this venture to fruition.

Roger W. Jones: Drill Instuctor
U. S. Marine, One of My Heroes.

His opening line cued raucous, classic laughter on the first day of Marine Corps Boot Camp, Platoon 297, Parris Island, South Carolina, October 7, 1965.

"I'm 180 pounds of Baltimore asshole. If anyone wants to kick it, just LEAP right on up here!" The emphasis on "leap" was an octave higher than the rest of the invitation. One recruit from New Jersey did just that: Arthur L. Linderman. He walked to the center of the "squad bay" (barracks) to take the offer. There ensued a short grappling session where "Jonesie" grabbed him by the groin and "stacking swivel" (i.e. neck) and launched him head first into the 30-gal. trash can stationed at the center of our ever so elegant living quarters. After the laughter died down from the remaining 80 members of our recruit platoon, Sgt. Jones quietly intoned:

"Next!"

There were no further challengers. Follow an old Corps mantra: Don't volunteer! Lindeman had no injuries except his pride and became one of the most "squared-away" Marines to graduate some 11-weeks later. If I had to cite the three men in my life who had the most impact, I would start with my father (Charles Eugene), Catholic priest Rev.

David Lajoie (Society of Mary, Marist Fathers) the second, then "Jonesie." Remember that 1965 was just a year removed from the passage of the Civil Rights Act that shattered a host of barriers to the integration of American society. The armed services trumped the sublime idiocy of segregation during the Truman administration but social (de facto) segregation still prevailed in the old South, especially in South Carolina. The Marine Corps Recruit Depot at Parris Island was one of the islands where true integration was the required norm and the armed services were the only institutions that actively incorporated minorities. So Sgt. (E-5) Roger W. Jones was one of the pioneer Americans who went from "Colored Person" to "Negro" to "Afro-American" to "Black," all in one lifetime. But, most of all, he was the penultimate U. S. Marine! I hope he's still alive and survived to become an "African-American." He is a Marine who needed no hyphenation. As of 2016, he would be 88.

My bet is that he is still a lean, mean 180 pounds.

At age 37 he was in better shape than all of us recruits who ranged from 17 to 20. Yet he led us on every, daily 3-mile run both morning and afternoon and, like all Marine drill instructors, never asked us to perform something that he couldn't do himself. Marine Corps DIs are like that, an amazing cross-breed of monasticism and "stud." "Jonesie" was my personal boot camp hero. Although some of my peers in Platoon 297 in 1965 didn't understand much of the reason for the exercise of discipline with seemingly inane rituals, repetition and drills, I was savvy enough to fall in step. Thus I rarely incurred the "specialized" attention a drill instructor would anoint a recruit sporting an attitude incongruent with that of a United States Marine. I only fell prey to that singular inspiration once. That was on day three of the first week of training. When the physical training instructor announced that the mandatory Physical Fitness Test three-mile run would begin immediately because of the accelerated commitment to the Vietnam War, Private Fitch intoned from the back of the platoon formation: "Three (bleeping) miles! Call me a cab!"

Standing in back of me, however, was the Senior Drill Instructor, R. J. Deffes Jr. and he was not amused by my editorial comment. Thus I endured some of his specialized attention for the next two days, did a ton of push-ups, stood "fire watch" for the next three nights in the barracks and made all the runs, much to my intense delight and surprise. That's how we all learned at sundry points to "watch, look and listen." But at all costs: Shut up until asked to sound off! See the character portrayed by real Gunnery Sergeant and now actor R. Lee Ermey in the film "Full Metal Jacket." Except for that supremely idiot script digression of the suicide in the middle of the film, it is as close to reality of 12-weeks at Parris Island and Sgt. Jones as I can cite. What every current and forever Marine will tell you, the drill instructors seemed to know every twist, turn and gossip about you. It's truly uncanny. They are gossip magnets all. Several anecdotes will suffice to enlighten.

I confided to one other recruit that I was a Roman Catholic seminarian for some years and opted not for the priesthood the preceding January. When I left the seminary, I contracted that virulent disease "1-A" that afflicted American males from 18 to 26 in the mid-60s. It was a terminal illness. My Uncle Sam decided to induct me into the U. S. Army in October of 1965. I beat him to the punch and enlisted in the Corps 1 October of the same year. Arrival at the Parris Island resort followed on October 7. Some days later, on a Sunday morning after church services (the only time you had to yourself!), Sgt. Jones was with us in the squad bay as we did all those Marine things like spit-shine shoes, clean brass, recite our 11 General Orders ad nauseam and rearrange our foot lockers for the 57th time.

"Jonesie" had this quirky habit of always having a pipe in his mouth on which he always chewed but never smoked. It was one of those funny images that will always make me smile until death as he would tease you with these big, rolling brown eyes and a smile that always ran from PI to Charleston, SC.

One Sunday, after returning from the chapel, I was the object of that famed command: "Private Fitch. LEAP right on up here!" to the center of the squad bay. Standing squarely at attention: As loudly as I could muster, the bellowed response followed. "Private Fitch, reporting as ordered. Sir!"

"Private Fitch, I understand that, in civilian life, you were going to become a 'man of God'?"

"Yes, sir!"

With this endearing grin on his face, he then said:

"Well I don't fuck with God! Get out of here."

The laughter that followed had its intended effect to loosen us up and begin to see all Marines, even the more profane ones, as very feeling human beings. The drill instructors apparently decided at that point that I was sufficiently self-disciplined to pass through the filter of training harassment imposed on those with continuing attitudes. And our platoon had more than its allocated share. The traditional team of three DIs turned their attention to the more incorrigible others of the famed 81 of Platoon 297, several of whom from Baltimore were under court orders from sundry judges to enlist. The median education level of my boot camp platoon was 9th grade. And that's not a misprint. I was one of the two recruits who had been thrown out of college. Catholic University in Washington, D. C. had no further use for me with a 1.6 GPA and Georgetown University told George Tierney to get lost for a panoply of venial sins that, I believe, including a side betting business with a pool ring. Oh, to quote Colonel Kurtz: "The horror!"

Then there was the hysterical Sunday dialogue with Jonesie and a recruit who attended then 5th Avenue High School in my hometown of Pittsburgh, also named Jones. The recruit who then had to "Leap right on up here!" to the center of the squad bay was a "dark-green," future Marine with a bad lisp but a warm personality. While he was at 5th Avenue, he apparently had a side business with several of the girls in his class. I guess you could say he was a "procurer" of social clients for the ladies, sort of a "Hookers.com" kind of business. Well, Jonesie couldn't resist!

With the private at attention, Roger W. Jones began his combination of interrogation and homily. The wry smile hinted at the cross-examination about to ensue.

"Private, I understand in civilian life that you were a 'businessman'?" Then came the ambush: "I want you to tell the other privates all about the (pause for effect)....the business."

Well Private Jones' lisp kicked in and he began. The stuttered response of the 5th-Avenue recruit only encouraged Jonesie more. The DI interrupted the narrative with tantalizing questions about the details, the exchange rates and nuances of "the services offered." I have rarely laughed that hard in my adult life. Without demeaning the recruit, Jonesie lead him through a comic cross-examination that drained us all. Several minutes later, when the laughter finally became too much, DI Jones re-appeared "in camera" with a seemingly serious last question.

"Recruit, do you need any business partners when you get out of the Corps?"

A Marine as "squared away" as Sgt. Jones would today be a retired Sergeant Major. Rank was much more difficult to attain in the "Old Corps" of the '50s and '60s. Limited promotions and rank followed the drawdown after the 1953 truce that suspended the Korean War. I'm sure he also fought through the prejudice of the newly-integrated armed services. After all, 1965 was fewer than 20 years removed from the integration ordered during the Truman administration. So it was not unusual in 1965 to find squared-away, career sergeants who today would attain promotion to Gunnery Sergeant, First Sergeant or Sergeant Major. Jones had been in the Corps for 18 years and was still an E-5. And he had his act together. Remember, to a Marine, the "Old Corps" is what it was like 20 minutes before he or she enlisted. It's all on the perspective of the time you served. I personally would have nominated Jones for Sergeant Major of the whole U. S. Marine Corps......then or now.

And, as a footnote to history, the Korean War is not "over." It's a truce without end that may once again ensnare Marines et al. again….some six decades later. It's 2016. This time it's the grandson at the helm of the DPRK (Democratic Peoples' Republic of Korea, a.k.a. North Korea).

But the most enduring Jones quote that I have carried since 1965 ought to be inscribed on the foreheads of all the politically-correct idiots who think the Marine Corps and our military brethren are some sort of social experiment. They don't get to play with national security with an agenda that looks to incorporate those traditionally excluded from whatever American subgroup they promote from gay to transvestite to transgendered and now women "grunts." There's a reason boot camp is and should be ferociously tough and Corps training is not for the faint of heart….and shouldn't be. Marines are not boy scouts and both my trips to two wars never seemed like a week-long camp-out at Valley Forge. Heed the "Words of Roger W. Jones!"

"If you can't tolerate the artificial pressure of boot camp, you will die in combat!"

Having done both boot camp and two wars since 1967, Roger W. Jones is indeed the "sage of Baltimore."

My enduring, second-to-last image of this magnificent Marine was graduation day when he accompanied us by bus to Infantry Training Regiment at Camp Lejeune, NC. It was the first time we all were in "Alphas," the green uniform that is the standard even today throughout the Corps. Graduation day is the first time that anyone on the training staff will address you as "Marine." Heretofore, it was "recruit" or whatever derogatory term today deemed politically incorrect by the politically-correct morons who inhabit Federal bureaucracy. Patrick's personal, risible favorites were "maggot" and "scumbag." Today the drill instructor would face a court-martial for such transgression. After all, we don't want to puncture the fragile, frail egos of future warriors we pay to kill, maim and destroy the enemies of the United States! When we egressed the buses, Sgt. Jones shook all our hands, called us Marines and stood there crying his eyes out. It remains one of the most profoundly emotional moments of my entire adult life. It ranks right up there with my father's funeral at 15 and there on Pennsylvania Avenue in November, 1963 as I watched the JFK caisson pass by en route to Arlington. Jones stood there, plush with the pride of a parent detaching us forward to assume the violent missions for which he trained us. Drill instructors become very attached to their recruits and that defines the lifetime brotherhood the Corps is. His tears are a part of my life today. Jones and Khe Sanh daily define who I am. Fifty- plus years later, he is a part of my rich routine of memories that always buoy my soul. What a remarkable human being.

My last, sustained image of Roger Jones was at Dong Ha Combat Base, Republic of Vietnam, in February, 1967. It was my third day "in-country." I suddenly heard a loud, booming command from 30 yards "to my six."

"Fitch, drop down and give me 20!"

After the 20, I jumped up to give him a warm, fraternal hug. God Bless then Staff Sergeant Roger W. Jones (artillery: 0830) and the U. S. Marine Corps. His words, training and mentoring directly enhanced my survival skills during a horrendous combat experience with 1st Battalion, 26th Marines at Khe Sanh Combat Base and the Tet Offensive of 1968. He changed my life and those of many other U. S. Marines. If he ever decided to give up his allegedly professed atheism and became a Catholic, I'd declare him a saint.

If alive today, he's a national treasure. If deceased, he's Sergeant of-the-Guard at the Celestial Gate. And you had best pass his inspection and muster even before God checks you saintly resume.....or the re-unification of body and soul will begin with a passel of mandatory push-ups. St. Roger of Baltimore is the patron saint of several platoons of U. S. Marines. Jones: tears; patriot; brother!

Thirteen Months, Ten Days, Eight Hours and 35 Minutes!

One of the common irritations that beset some Americans during the Vietnam War was the difference in "tours" between the Army and Navy personnel. Soldiers spent 12 months in country while Marines did 13. In some perverse logic employed by the Perfumed Princes of the Pentagon (a phrase coined by author Col. David Hackworth), Marines came by ship while soldiers flew their way to war. I went to 'Nam on the U.S. N. S. Gordon, an old WW II troop transport tub. I took 28 days as we boarded in San Diego, took a side trip to Oakland with a school of porpoise and then headed west. With perfunctory stops at Vung Tau and Cam Ranh Bay on the south coast of the country, we unloaded at Danang.

That's when I knew we weren't going to win the war.

If America had any illusions or doubts about how committed the population of then South Vietnam was, mine was and remained shattered on Day 1 of that sunny February morning.

There lining our debarkation route from the ocean front to the 3rd Marine Division "reception center" were scores of Vietnamese hocking, cajoling, or selling everything from soap (Tide being the favorite) to boots. It was an early rendition of Wal Mart, except all the stuff was likely intercepted, pilfered, secured or stolen from the military PX system. And these were our "friends" that we were there to help save them from Uncle Ho Chi Minh and the eventual Communist takeover? It hit me like the heat that this strategy that we do the heavy lifting while the Vietnamese were in support was a hot crock of water buffalo manure. It defined dysfunctional. The urban dwellers on the coastal cities seemed detached from the central government in Saigon and rural Vietnamese were pre-occupied with daily survival. So as early as that February of 1967, it was apparent to this gunslinger that the "rules of engagement" already doomed and mangled the effort to really win the war. If the South Vietnamese wouldn't take the lead in their own civil war, why the hell were we there in the first place? It's the same with the closure of Haiphong Harbor, the North Vietnamese main supply route from the "Rooskies." Why didn't we do it? It's a question that has hung over an entire generation of Vietnamese and American veterans who still tally the casualty count and attendant horrific cost.

After processing, I posted to the 1st Battalion, 9th Marines at Dong Ha. During the "briefing" and dispersal of orders, I asked the attendant first sergeant why 1/9 needed a court-reporter (my original Military Occupational Specialty) given the fact they had sustained heavy casualties and ongoing, relentless combat near the old Demilitarized Zone between North and South Vietnam. Thus their nickname: "The Walking Dead."

"No, Lance Corporal, you are foremost a grunt (0311)."

Resigned to said, I woke up the next morning in a reception tent with a group of "chu hoys," pronounced CHEW-HOY, Viet Cong guerillas who surrendered to the South Vietnamese government and repatriated. That led to my first cross-cultural foray next morning when I went outside the tent and began to shave with four Vietnamese men about my age who sat in that defecation squat position that I have never managed to mimic. They sat around mystified at what I was doing. Vietnamese rarely developed facial hair of any consequence until old age. You wouldn't see Ho Chi Minh's beard on anyone under 30. But then they shifted the conversation to women, girlfriends and.......sex. It's a universal obsession.

I could only laugh at the conversation that followed.

They spoke no English. I spoke no Vietnamese.

But they then produced pictures of their girlfriends and all attested with very clear hand motions that all four girls were "No. 1 'Boom-booms!'" Virginity was in short supply with that crew as they were fascinated by the picture of my then girlfriend with her glasses, an uncommon sight in Vietnam '67. They had a rollicking good time describing the girlfriends' "talent" with closed captions. I knew what they meant and I learned my first nasty Vietnamese word for cunnilingus and the requisite gesture used to convey it. Not much different from anything you could hear from an average college undergraduate in a dorm setting. Welcome to Vietnam!

But, alas, it didn't break my heart that my orders were modified the very next day and I was sent "down south" to Phu Bai with the 1st Battalion, 26th marines with whom I remained for the duration of the tour. Older Marines always ask me if I suffer from Unit Alzheimers as the 5th Marine Division was the mother unit of the 26th Marine regiment. The 5thMarDiv was not "stood up" in toto for the war, only the individual regiment with its three battalions as the division was deactivated after WWII. Thus the 3rd Marine Division attached the regiment to its core and it became 3rd Marine Division (Reinforced).

Not long afterwards we moved to Hill 55 west of Danang where a sniper team tried and failed to kill me and several other Marines that spring. A firefight ensued.

The perimeter bunkers along and surrounding the hill top had roofs and open firing positions much hunting blinds used during deer season here in Kentucky. The bunkers were designed as 4-man fighting holes with two asleep per four-hour shifts and two on watch. About 0200 that morning in April, another Marine from Beaver Falls, PA (Peter Rubus) and I had just lain in the two cots inside the bunker after the first watch when a torrent of rounds shattered the illusion of sleep. This was my reaction as the rounds went swirling 8-12 inches above our heads:

"Mr. Rubus, I believe we're being fired upon!"

"Mr. Fitch, I believe you're right!"

Thus I grabbed the land line and reported the continuing attack to the battalion officer of the watch.

"Place two well-aimed rounds at the source of the incoming," he said. Another rookie mistake by a rookie lieutenant!

We could see the automatic weapon firing at us from the base of the hill approximately 35-40 yards away. So Patrick jumped into the adjacent trench line and hurled three anti-personnel grenades at the weapon's team. That coupled with an M-60 machine gun at the bunker adjacent opened up to my left, so the noise accelerated along with dozens of spent rounds with our new M-16A1s ("You can tell it's Mattel! It's swell!") The outgoing fusillade expended roughly 200 rounds, true to the axiom: "When in doubt, empty your magazine!" Well the incoming firing ceased as the Viet Cong intruders slipped away into the night but they got the hint. Not so the young lieutenant on watch. The phone in the bunker rang off its base. We gave it a very tardy response.

"What was that, Lance Corporal, didn't I tell you to place three well-aimed rounds?" That was in reference to the three grenades he obviously heard explode.

"Yes, sir, those were incoming, sir!"

So the lieutenant called a "red alert" and everybody was up and no one got any sleep.

Moral of the story: Never trust a second lieutenant who opines "in my experience" and issues a manifestly dumb order or a gunnery sergeant with a clipboard. A "butter bar" (2nd Lt.) has limited or no experience and the gunny is merely looking for "volunteers" for a shit detail.

So the Boy Scout Viet Cong achieved their mission of depriving an entire battalion of sleep and wasting several hundred rounds of perfectly good ammunition. It was a parable for the entire war!

The Cobra and Bill Jayne

Every hostile environment in a war zone has its own unique flavor, sustained threats and ambiguities to which you must adjust. The jungles of Southeast Asia are no exception. Unless you are fighting a war on the surface of the moon, you must account for topography, weather and animal life. Vietnam had and still has the best and worst of all three.

From alluring beaches to steaming mountains, take your pick. The country with less than 30 miles from coastline to Laos at its mid-section is rife with rats the size of French poodles to the incessant man-eating bugs that thought bug repellant was an aperitif dinner cocktail. Everything that crawls on the ground there is hazardous to your health. It amazes me that so many human beings adjusted so readily over the centuries. What follows in "Navy parlance!" is a sea story: "This ain't no shit, it really happened." That's always the opening graph of any tale told by a sailor drenched in hyperbole and sometimes alcohol.

During the combat lull during the summer of 1967, our TAOR (Tactical Area of Responsibility: The zone around Khe Sanh Combat Base) was eerily quiet like a serenity cap on a grenade. Pick your cliché:

Calm before the storm, night begets day or any other phrase that fits. They're all correct. Bravo Company, 1ˢᵗ Battalion, 26ᵗʰ Marine Regiment ran more than 100 patrols that summer with "no contact." And, if an enemy doesn't pick a fight with Marines, Marines will suffer the terminal purgatory of welcome boredom. Such was a day in July of that year when three of us then associated with the S-1 (administrative section) of the Headquarters and Service Company got the "day off" to do the mandatory weapons cleaning, laundry and "field day" the area around our bunker that I remember by the designation of "Hole 6." After transporting several buckets of water to our perimeter position, we would wash our utilities and socks, then put them on the perimeter concertina wire to dry. In 100-degree heat, that was not a problem. While one of us would watch the M-60 machine gun, the others would do their laundry. "Victor Charlie Snake" interrupted our chores. He was a lengthy 6-footer with a red ring around its neck. I opted to allow him to pass on with "a by your leave, sir!" and stay the hell away from our bunker.

Not so Bill Jayne.

Bill was and is a terminal comic now happily retired in North Carolina after a career stint in Federal civil service as a senior administrator of the Federal cemetery system throughout the world. You can catch him on Facebook nowadays to attest to the following. But, that summer, Bill was just bored and felt compelled to do what almost all junior Marines will do in similar circumstance: "Mess with da' snake!"

His combat choice of arms against this major herpetological threat was an "E-tool." That's the "entrenching tool" that all Marines carried with their packs to dig. It is one of those endearing, necessary items to create a "fighting hole" (not a foxhole) in the field. Upon re-issue of the set of "782" gear during my return to the reserve component, my wife dubbed the item as "that cute little shovel." Known affectionately as "Deuce gear," the collection includes the cartridge belt, helmet, bayonet, canteens, flak jacket and pack along with a first aid kit normally placed adjacent to the hip with a large sterile bandage for use if you, the carrier, sustained a major injury.

Bill's choice of arms was the E-tool and he began teasing the snake with with zest. While he did his best "Scaramouche" to challenge the snake with a simulated sword fight, the red-ringed serpent would have none of it. After all, it was a creature with a highly suspect Biblical past.

The viper reacted with vigor, curled into a tight ball, shot up three feet in the air and threw out a hood and hissed violently. Welcome to our first encounter with a cobra! The three of us remained outside the snake's striking area and watched with deprecating laughter as "William the Toreador" of snakes egged the snake to battle. Erring on the side of caution, I called over the Khe Sanh military land line to our Battalion Aid Station some three hundred yards away. I described the ensuing battle to the senior corpsman on watch. Forty-eight years later (now 2016), I still remember his risible response when I reported that we had a cobra on the perimeter.

"There are no cobras at this elevation in Vietnam, Marine."

For the geographically impaired, Khe Sanh Combat Base is and was about 5,500 elevated from sea level. That's about the altitude difference between the desert floor at Palm Springs to city of Idyllwild above it overlooking the city of Hemet, CA.

"Well, send Dr. (Harvey) DeMaag (the senior medical officer of 1/26) out here," I said, "because we can confirm that a cobra is here."

"Well, cut the head off and bring it to us so we can identify the species."

Well Bill Jayne won the contest and we delivered said trophy to the BAS for the confirmation. Yeah, Bill wacked a legitimately poisonous, deadly viper that only reminded us of the eternal hazard of the ground serpents around us.

What Marines will do to kill time!

It was day 148 of my tour. There were only 217 days left until return to the United States. And I still despise snakes, yet now live with a coterie of Copperheads here on our property in Kentucky. Today (June, 2015), I have a four-foot copperhead under my back deck that I am "hunting." He had the gall to come out this spring and plant his demonic ass in my wife's budding tomato plants. He escaped this time but I am now armed with a Mossberg 500. He's going to snake hell with the rest of his satanic buddies sometime this summer in 2015. I'll keep my audience apprised but I will harbor no copperheads as neighbors around my palace at Marine Barracks, Lone Oak, KY.

The Bru, Dan Rather and Wycliffe Bibles

During the lull, interregnum and prior to joining Bravo Company during the eternal Asian "monsoon" season of '67-'68, I spent several miserable nights on "listening posts," awaiting the expected arrival of the North Vietnamese 325B division. Their late arrival the next January was not unanticipated. An LP is a fire team of four sent forward of whatever the perimeter is of a combat base with a radio (maybe a land line) to alert the main detachment of the approaching enemy. These delightful sojourns were mostly cold, miserable and pretty bleeping scary. And, to defy the stereotype, night time during monsoon can be very cold, dropping to the low 50s with attendant rain so heavy that visual and auditory acuity blurred your ability to function at all. My mother even sent me "long johns" to fight the cold. There were none then in the 1/26 military inventory.

One of those enforced nights of misery stands out. Memory fades, however, as two images melded into one on a distant plain one Sunday dark AM.

Once in a while the LP would include one of the sentry dogs who work very well in some environments, less well in others like Vietnam where the range of humidity puts breeds like German Shepherds in severe distress. They can't do the necessary heat exchange as breeds with shorter hair like Doberman Pinchers. On one of those enforced assignments of misery, we had a K-9 "kraut" of said persuasion. About 0400, he got sick. You know how dogs retch it up like a starting pitcher before they vomit….and there's no mistaking what was about to happen next. The vomiting was loud and obnoxious.

You could have heard him from Quang Tri Province to Haiphong Harbor. The handler rightly said "We gotta' go back in the wire!" All three of the rest of the team concurred. On this particular LP, we had both a land line that we strung from the perimeter with wire to a box field phone along with a PRC-25 radio so we tried to alert the awaiting sentries of our return.

It was among the longest 100 yards of my young life. It could have been the 1,500 at Pickett's Gettysburg charge. Running was not an option. What a choice: Maybe shot by the NVA from behind or a U. S. Marine asleep on the job, suddenly startled, to whack you coming into camp.

The Marine in the bunker with the land line had fallen asleep. Combat does that. Exhaustion and fatigue can pre-curse death as well as a deadly frontal assault. After several failed attempts to rally the sentry, we opened up the "Prick-25" and had to loudly convey to the battalion HQ our dilemma with the dog. Minutes devolved into what seemed like an hour before a sentry team from battalion went to the reception bunker. Even a PRC-25 on "silent mode" is loud enough to announce your presence for almost 50 yards.

It was one of those "Oh, shit!" moments of impending doom where your testicles float north to your diaphragm. Suffice it to say, we made it back with no further incident, went to our bivouac tent, unloaded our gear as dawn approached, took our mess kits and went to the chow hall or what passed as one.

It was a T-shaped elevated, wooden structure with necessary screens all around daily breached by divisions of North Vietnamese flies sent by Ho Chi Minh special delivery. When food service followed, it often had an adjunct array of flies that made the attendant meal appear sprinkled with large grains of pepper. Spotted dehydrated eggs: A choice treat! Flies became the condiment.

Just as I traversed the hall onto the chow line accompanied by my requisite squad of flesh-eating insects, I encountered a vision. In front of me in the line was a very stunning, very pregnant, blonde white woman along with her husband. They were missionaries from the Wycliffe Bible Society who had been in Khe Sanh village for almost seven years. Their work among the Bru tribesmen was a combination of proselytizing, social work and scholarly documentation of the Bru dialect and language. The Bru are dark, almost the skin tone of Pakistanis and Indians. They have thick black hair and are genuinely handsome people. Unfortunately, they suffered rampant discrimination at the hands of the Vietnamese who, even today....whether they admit it or not, have a distinct bias against people with darker skin. The missionaries (John and Carolyn Miller) had totally integrated with the Bru locally and introduced everything from written language to personal hygiene. The first time I saw a young Bru teen at one of our "water buffaloes" inside the compound brushing his teeth with a tube of Colgate and a toothbrush, it drove home the point about how effective their work was and what good they did.

That morning mess hall apparition peaked my interest and, at a later point in the fall, we had a very slack work load in the S-1 (administration) and I once again "volunteered" to go on guard patrol with a contingent from CBS news led by Dan Rather. He was there to interview the Millers for the CBS nightly news with Walter Chronkite. So four of us "loaded up" and followed the CBS contingent to the village. We were "ready for Freddy!" with helmets, flak jackets and the whole regalia when we passed a "deuce-and-half" (2.5 ton standard truck) with Green Berets who lounged in the truck with just their "TO" weapons and no protective gear like they were going to the beach. We thus deduced that this "Rather Recon" was going to be a very safe foray.

And it was.

Rather went on with a lengthy interview that included the two young Miller children (both under six years of age) who had both been born at Khe Sanh. During our noon chow break, I was seated against the front truck tire (always have something solid behind your back) when this gorgeous little Bru girl about five years old sat down next to me. She had these gooey brown eyes and a short, flip, stylish haircut that showed some adult paid real attention to this kid's needs. Although she spoke limited English, her smile spoke volumes and she could recognize all the elements of the four C-ration kits we had broken out to eat. She pointed right to the peanut butter can along with the cracker cans, licked her lips and made a hand gesture for me to wait.

Two minutes later she returned with a bunch of bananas, sat down again and implored me to open the can with my "John Wayne" (a small can opener that came with every C-Ration mean). I then took my K-bar, sliced the bananas and she and I shared the lunch meal. Thus she introduced me to one my favorite snack sins: peanut butter and bananas. Her English was flawed but she spoke fluent C-ration! Right after that, she secured her toothbrush and the water from one of my canteens for another cross-cultural experience. She had a tube of toothpaste and impeccably white teeth that matched her smile.

Today, if she survived the war, she'd be about 50 years old.

I'd love to meet her again. She touched my heart and reminded me that the Vietnam War has not ended for some....and that includes the Bru.

Thomas Allerton Meade, USMC, Cpl

October 17, 1947-February 6, 1968

Artillery, rocket, mortar attack

Khe Sanh Combat Base, Republic of South Vietnam

U.S. Marine Tom Meade died at 20. So why does his death still linger in my psyche in 2016? Mostly because the country doesn't know his name nor do they care. His "placa" (en Espanol) remains on my wall of military history. He joins the long list of Americans committed to "overseas contingents," as the current crop of executive grad students in DC call them, who will die for obscure, ill-defined commitments under the banner of patriotism. They are the true one-per-centers.

Tom's summary was stark. He was an "0141:" S-1 administrator, born on 17 October 1947, a Roman Catholic, single, from Orange, New Jersey. What the "placa" doesn't tell you angers me and has for more than 45 years. Tom was a committed Marine who coined the phrase "Hippiecrit" to describe those who declined to serve. Prior to my transfer to Bravos, 1/26, I was the only court-reporter for the 1st Battalion, 26th Marines. It was a job I relished like a weekly colonoscopy. I then joined Bravo Company of the same battalion in

December, 1967 and remained there as a field radio operator until my tour of duty ended in March, 1968. Thirteen months, ten days and 35 minutes later outside the continental United States (CONUS the acronym)! The now retired commanding officer of Bravo Company then was Kenneth W. Pipes. After conversation with him June 15, 2016, he still remains another one of my heroes. Forty-five years and counting! The men of Ken Sanh/Sahn are still my most necessary brothers. We lived through the dire straits of raw combat and most American will never know how abiding those connections remain.

Thus this is the tribute here to Tom Meade. Only those of us who remember him, along with his twin brother and family have any concern for those who drop in combat. It is the ultimate argument for all of us to "get out of Afghanistan sooner rather than 2020!" Weeks after Tom died, I received a wrenching letter from his father asking HOW he died. We were still at Khe Sanh and the siege was at its zenith. I spared him the gory details as I thought it would do nothing to suppress his sorrow, or despair. This is the first time I've written about it and it remains the ugly, painful truth. During one of our many violent artillery and mortar attacks we sustained, Tom took shelter in one of our many makeshift bunkers along with other Marines from Delta Company, 1/26. His next rash move would end his life.

Tom had an old Brownie "Instamatic" camera with which he wanted to take some photo shots and send them to his twin brother then stationed at Headquarters, Marine Corps. He never made it. A Russian 130-mm rocket landed almost on top of him near the entrance of the bunker. The body bag's contents were that remained: A left arm with his signature wristwatch. Ironically, his father wrote, it was his twin brother who first learned of the death as his assignment was in a section that processed death notices from the field at Headquarters, Marine Corps.

Much of the reason why I today question the extended commitment to the corrupt governments of Afghanistan and Iraq is the parallel to our similar retreat from the Republic of South Vietnam. All that emanated from the Tom Meade trauma. How many of our best must die for the nebulous, vain aim of "nation-building"? I re-entered the Marine Corps reserve in 1987 and deployed with them to the Gulf War before it didn't look like the cakewalk it became. I had married Anita a mere four years before (at 41: 1st and only wife!) and my daughter, Adriana, was just born in September, 1990. I was 45.....and still a sergeant (E-5). The return to the Marine Corps was a spiritual journey. Marines and military veterans still remain the most trustworthy subset of people I know and the limited subset of people I completely trust. If you haven't been through it, it's both difficult to explain and with which to identify. Once crossed, that line can never be retraced.

I still have the official summary of Tom's death posted on my hallway here in Kentucky....and when we were in California. Every day I pass it, and the words remind me of God, Corps and country a la Douglas MacArthur. The trouble with the bulk of elected civilians who have rarely served anyone but themselves from Lyndon Baines forward is septic. That disdain for sacrifice that Tom and others have made is only remembered by about half the country. That augurs poorly for our future as a nation. The rest are at the mall or hyperventilating over their I-pads, I-phones and any internet toy that suppresses conversation. Tom was right: The "Hippiecrits" now run the show! And to conclude this ode to a valiant Marine who died too early. Patriotism ought to have more adherents than just the brotherhood of our military as the cult of death now emanating with ISIS threatens to destroy not only us but Christian and western civilization.

For five years, when I taught at West Valley High School in Hemet, Calif., I created and hosted a one-day Vietnam War Symposium every year for the juniors of all the U. S. History classes. We opened the event with Bill Coutourie's documentary film "Letters from Vietnam" that featured a host of narrating actors with big-time film resumes. Then we would break into smaller classroom groups with actual Vietnam vets whose stories were a lesson in real life. The history detailed was sometimes graphic and blunt but the guests were always well-received by the students eager for firsthand knowledge and insight. Their stories sometimes "freaked out" some of our faculty members who objected to the true stories of death in combat. Almost always in the "wrap-up" sequence at the end of the day in the school theater, there would always be some wise-ass male member of the assembled, junior class knuckleheads with the compulsive need to "push our buttons." Every year, one of the adolescent members of the wannabe intelligentsia would ask me or others of the guests the same question: "Hey, Mr. Fitch, how many people (and I'm cleaning it up here!), how many enemy did you kill?"

For the first three years of the program, I declined to answer, ignored the question and suggested the same to my guests. The KIA count was not the point of the presentation. Finally, however, tiring of the crass grab of immaturity, I gave one punk the honest answer in year four. And the narrative in years four and five went the same way.

"Do you want to know how many died from the air strikes I called over the radio with my senior FAO (forward air observer) Hank Norman or how many face-to-face?"

Both years, on cue, some wise ass (always a male) would ask.

"Ok, with the air strikes?"

"Probably several hundred."

"Ok, how about face-to-face?"

"Two"

"Waddya kill 'em with?"

"M-16 A-1!"

Then there would be this embarrassing, pregnant pause with nervous giggling.

"How do you feel about that, Mr. Fitch?"

"Better than they do. They're dead and I'm here with you."

But I would trade all that history, the siege and the Vietnam Symposiums just to have Tom Meade back with me on my back deck here in Kentucky, telling lies, sucking down a few iced, adult beverages and just being here. Guess that will just have to wait until we've checked in at the Celestial Guard Shack with the First Sergeant (St. Peter). Marines already know the streets there are safe.

An Intrusive Memory
25 Feb. 68 to 30 Days in the Sun

The red dirt was the carpet of a landscape cape sculpted with torqued debris after six weeks living in a human trash dump guarded by healthy, well-fed rats and a division of flies. Yet the Soviet gifts of incoming artillery were like Hallmark Cards, the gifts that kept on giving. On average, postcards from General Vo Nyugen Giap averaged about 1,400 a day. Addressed to no one in particular, "incoming" was only accurate if you were its mailed recipient. Welcome to Khe Sanh in Quang Tri Province in the Central Highlands near the oxymoron of the old Demilitarized Zone, a plateau few Americans knew and even fewer could spell in the winter of 1968. At 5,500 feet elevation, it has two seasons: Humid and monsoon. Temperatures fluctuated often more than 50 degrees Fahrenheit per diem to top the chart with more than 100 during the sultry summer months. Then it would plunge into the low 50s at night. During monsoon (circa November through February), long-johns and slickers were in order to combat rain in sheets thickly bundled that nighttime visibility was three to five feet. So came another 25th of February, the eve of my 23rd birthday and, as one of the oldest Marines so confined, what appeared to be another annoying round of the 325th North Vietnamese Army Division's annoying attempt to fill more body bags. Kill us they could but their real design was to restrict us from confronting them and kicking their ass from Quang Tri to Haiphong Harbor. Pentagon fear of further casualties put the 26th Marines in a shooting gallery that could only match General Giap's trap. We wanted to fight but the NVA merely wanted to confine our movement and options.

They succeeded........for 76 days!

That's small consolation for the families of the 325 service members who died near Lang Vei and Khe Sanh on that infamous combat base along with some 1,100 wounded over that four-month period. Argue the figures, you may, as did the sycophants from the Department of Defense who dutifully marched over to Capitol Hill, then genuflected at the feet of the Congressional cretins. It wasn't a conspiracy but ineptitude of the part of the reporting American press that distorted the reported numbers inaccurately. But the chaplain of the 1st Battalion, 26 Marines, Rev. Ray Stubbe, was much more precise than the journalism wonks of the major news outlets. Their inability to fudge the exam count only confirmed their room-temperature IQs and the joke of the "5 O'Clock Follies" in Saigon. Stubbe, however, kept an exact body count of every American whose body left the Khe Sanh Combat Base and his figures blatantly contradicted the often convoluted rationale the press used to report the dead and wounded. The casualty figures segregated into three "campaigns" used to define the 77-day siege of the former French artillery base. It coddled the dead into a time line before Jan. 21, the actual siege and the aftermath. But it was a maladroit count under the pressure of deadline. If you had a 20 percent casualty rate in your unit, that normally would mandate a commander relieved of duty. But then Col. David Lowends was one first-class Commanding Officer of a regiment whose hands were tied by both the Military Assistance Comand Vietnam (MACV) and McNamara's Band of Whiz Kids in the White House. He deserved better. We all deserved better.

Although the North Vietnamese forward artillery spotters had a well-defined shooting gallery like some morose table game board, their initial hits only confirmed what we already knew. They hit both ammunition dumps on each end of the flight line early on the morning of 21 January. Thereafter it was random and the counter-fire from our three artillery batteries of 105-mm cannon and a fourth of a battery of 155mm. The counter fire was so precise that it shut down most of the incoming for the bulk of the "work day." How did that work?

Behold the application of high school geometry! It was comically simple.

Take a compass and "shoot an azimuth (direction)" from where an incoming round approaches. That is…point the compass at the sound and direction of the incoming round. Then have a second Marine/spotter at an alternate location and shoot a similar azimuth toward the same round. Now you have an intersection where the two arms of the scalene triangle made by both azimuths cross at the point of incoming origin. Then radio that data on the target to one of our two artillery batteries. That cued the counter-fire on a plotting board and the reply was nearly instant for Ho Chi Minh and friends. Now contemporary "gun grunts" have computers that do the computation. Unlike the yelling and loud repetition of target co-ordinates, current FDICs (Fire Direction Control Centers) have mostly the tapping noise on keyboards or IPads with "fire mission" input information. But the net effect is still the same. If you really want to get your "jollies," just take out the whole grid square (1000 square meters) at the targeted intersection and obliterate it. Fire for effect: 16 rounds HE (high explosive)! Then give the second command, used only on the radio for artillery: "Repeat"! Next to sex, the rush I got from calling artillery on the NVA was almost pre-orgasmic. Adrenaline does that. "Fuckin'-A!" We were good at it and the NVA knew it.

That's partially why their incoming rocket rounds had no specific pattern because they launched them from dummy pads and then split. Call it a "drive-by" artillery strike! They knew we would send them an immediate response and we did so with much love and affection. That birthday eve, however, saw more than 1,500 rounds poured onto our little speck of heaven that was about the size of an average American high school campus. That's a lot of holes in the football field. They were serious and so were we. That's where I awoke on that morning at 0730 just off the night watch I'd served from 0200 to 0600. It was about 0730 (ante meridiem) and the manure had hit the spreader. Thus Corporal Patrick J. Fitch was about to become an unintended part of infamous history. What follows are my observations of the ensuing day that even today define my approach to life.

Second Lieutenant Don Jacques came to my attention when he first reported to 1/26 several months earlier when I was confined to the battalion S-1 (administrative office) in a role I despised as the battalion court-reporter. Jacques had just finished Marine Corps Officer Basic School at Quantico and still very green and "gung ho." Although the work of a Judge Advocate General (JAG) officer or enlisted is essential, I found it tedious, boring and dysfunctional in a combat zone. To further enhance the tedium, they put me in the S-1 administration tent where I was drafted into clerical work. I felt like an indentured servant in a rat maze and badly wanted to go to a line company. Enter the newly-minted lieutenants, all three of them. Jacques was the most loquacious. I don't remember the specific exchange but, as recalled by now retired Col. John M. Kaheny, then a lieutenant and one of longest-serving officers in 1st Battalion, 26th Marines, said I was a little "flippant" with the new lieutenants in very clean utilities.

"Hey, Corporal, send me to the company with the most action," Jacques said. He actually did say that. That's a November Sierra! (Translation: "No shit!")

None of us "veterans" of the life in Quang Tri Province were real anxious to accommodate rookie officers with stars in eyes for heroism. "If it's action you want, Lieutenant, go back to Quantico. We're not interested here." Yeah, that sounds sound like me circa 1968. I had no time for ambitious future recipients of the Medal of Honor. Truth in the narrative is I do not remember the incident, but it is true to my form. Kaheny brought it to my attention years later. It doesn't take long to become crusty or "salty" in combat. And the Marines I knew damn sure didn't want to collect the "Trifecta" of Purple Hearts that then led to an automatic return to "the World" and termination of your tour in Southeast Asia. The tragic events of months later were a sad underscore to unrequited ambition. Then Captain Kenneth W. Pipes, who commanded the Headquarters & Service Company of which I was part, became commander of Bravo Company sometime around Thanksgiving of 1967. Thus I deemed it time for a fourth shot at release from secretarial/administrative prison.

Fourth "request mast." "Please, sir, get me the hell out!" This time he greased the necessary skid because my future replacement had just arrived and it just buttressed my argument: "No battalion needs two legal clerks!"

Pipes correctly concurred and I quietly shifted to the battalion headquarters in November 1967where I went through a crash course in field radio operations. Minimal proficiency attained, I shifted to the command bunker of Bravo Company, a stark, hexagonal, concrete building leftover from the U. S. Special Forces during earlier commitments to then South Vietnam. Previously used as an artillery base by the French prior to their disaster at Dien Bien Phu, Khe Sanh was also a harbinger of our own eventual exit. The French defeat and the eventual partition into North and then South Vietnam followed in 1954. The American withdrawal in 1972 then pre-cursed the collapse of the then Republic of South Vietnam and the country's communist reunification in 1975.

The famed 77-day Siege of Khe Sanh during the 1968 Tet Offensive began for us locally on the combat base proper at exactly 0535, Jan. 21 when the incoming rounds hit the artillery ammunition dump about 50 yards from the tent where I was still "bunked." Although military historians quibble about the beginning and end of the "siege," it was only real for us when your anal aperture slammed shut with the arrival of the initial "incoming," one of the dirtiest words in the lexicon of combat. I grabbed my M-16 A-1 (Just like American Express: Never leave home without it!) and scrambled toward the makeshift bunker adjacent to our tent and suddenly realized: "I left my glasses!" Maybe that's not a big deal for some, but my vision was (and remains) so poor that I cannot be drafted into the military. That came to my attention when I was with the 2nd Air Naval Gunfire Company at Camp Lejeune and reported for a flight physical so I could go to "jump school" at Fort Benning, GA. The Navy Battalion Surgeon delivered the bad news.

"LCpl Fitch, you don't see well enough to go to jump school.....or even be drafted. You eyesight is 20/200, 20/400!" Two weeks later I received orders to Vietnam. I went back to the Battalion Aid Station at Courthouse Bay, Camp Lejeune and then asked the same battalion surgeon, a Navy lieutenant, if somehow my ocular deficiency precluded deployment to the war zone. He chuckled and delivered the prognosis. "It doesn't work that way, Marine." I remained too blind to jump out of a perfectly good airplane but sufficiently visual to wade through an unforgiving, "double-canopy" jungle. Maybe they needed to issue M-16s with red tips so we could find the curbs that demarked the rice paddies. Sixteen years in the Corps with two wars on my resume (Vietnam & the Gulf), my vision remains equally impaired. Today I would evoke laughter at the recruiter's office. Would the military today reject a candidate with a Braille keyboard who could process an artillery strike from Tampa Bay, FL to a drone in Helmund Province, Afghanistan?

Ponder that.

But the day before my 23rd birthday, 1968, started out, as do most combat traumas, with utter, boring routine. I had just left a four-hour radio watch and moved several feet from the leftover French bunker to a "barracks" bunker of sandbags for some sleep. Fatigue can be just as big a killer in combat as a stray round and it was something from which we all suffered. Suddenly the cacophony of deafening gunfire interrupted shortly around 0800. Instinctively I ran to the CO's side with my radio (affectionately called a "Prick-25" for the PRC-25). Don't ask what the jargon means. I've forgotten. What loomed to our immediate west, fewer than two hundred meters away was a firefight where 2nd Lt. Jacques was victim to one the oldest of combat ploys. Two North Vietnamese regulars were "diddy-bopping" (walking) calmly south on the dirt road west of our position southward toward the village of Khe Sanh then under heavy assault by the same NVA division. Surrounded in the village proper, separate from our combat base surrounding the airfield, was a contingent of U. S. Army Special Forces along with a contingent of indigenous mercenaries, some of whom I had met prior to the siege.

My only sustaining memory of them was that they were better equipped with newer "782 deuce" gear including flak jackets, canteens, cartridge belts, first-aid kits and the other ancillary equipment that we Marines couldn't get. That and the fact they had a stridently proficient command of English obscenity and profanity that could make even the most hardened mother superior of your average convent blush to crimson.

In his haste to secure these meandering NVA as prisoners, Jacques ordered his lead squad forward, straight into what must have been a battalion-size ambush.

And there is no other polite way to describe what followed. For almost eight hours: It was a deafening exchange of the best and worst of combat. A second platoon from the company then exited the perimeter wire to assist. They too were pinned down and every element in the Marine inventory focused on the battlefield at hand right in front of us. A light Army 40-mm "duster" armored vehicle then followed up to the wire and began firing overhead cover. That was supplemented by at least one "Ontos" I saw, a small tracked-vehicle sporting six 105-mm rockets that also lit up the area where the NVA had sprung the ambush. The Ontos almost looked like a kid's toy but it was Mattel married to lethal. It had six 105-mm recoilless rifle tubes, three mounted on each side of the vehicle originally designed as an anti-tank weapon. It was about the size of a small, genetically modified John Deere farm tractor. The 105-mm artillery battery within our wire also began a series of zero-degree, loping fire of artillery shells toward the NVA positions. Add our 81-mm company mortar batteries and the NVA may have scored first but the return fire was equally so, both effective and brutal. The damage to Bravo, 1/26, however, was already done and it was severe. Radio communication was nil as either the operators were down or the radios inoperative.

Pipes then ordered me along with a protective fire team (four Marines) as part of an ad hoc addition to the extraction team into the fray. After a radio check where I went through the requisite radio checks within the company headquarters some 30 yards away, we exited the company line at a wire gate near the base garbage dump on the west end of the base home to hundreds of empty C-rations cans and assorted collective junk centralized for sanitary purpose. What it had really become was an eyesore colony of flies. A road (actually a dirt alley) adjacent to the dump also bordered an anti-tank minefield placed there in a rapid hurry when intelligence "passed the word" that the NVA had acquired these small, amphibious tanks. We never saw one but cautionary paranoia prevailed. Most of the mines were visible to the naked eye and the extraction team maneuvered around the dump and the minefield. "Murphy" then assumed command of the operation. The dump was in a small, declining revetment that cancelled the signal from my radio to anyone….even though I could see to whom we wanted to talk. So there we were, standing in the midst of a firefight with a 15-pound "hood ornament" on my back with an antenna that may as well should have had a flag embossed with "Shoot me!" flapping in the breeze.

Then transpired one of the more bizarre incidents of my adult life.

Jacque's platoon had a civilian still photographer embedded with his men long before "embedded" became a media cliché during the Iraq War. He (as I recall) had a trimmed beard and carried two 35-mm cameras around his neck while wandering around taking photographs like a tourist at the San Diego Zoo. We, however, were all much closer to the ground and thought this guy had lost his quota of cerebral brie and smoked too much of the "weed" favored by the local Bru tribesmen that they co-mingled with heroin poppies. In the middle of all this, he casually walked toward and through the minefield and the gate from which we had just exited to traverse around the mines. "Follow me, Marines," he yelled, "and walk in my footsteps."

Those of us in the extraction element watched him in perverse disbelief, then invited him loudly and rudely to self-fornicate. Marines do not "walk through minefields knowingly." I guess God watches over children, puppies, obnoxious fools and dumb-ass journalists. He qualified as a first-class idiot who took the photograph of the then dying Lt. Jacques that appeared less than a week later on the cover of Newsweek Magazine. Jacques was hit by bullets twice in the groin and was bleeding to death as four Marines carried his wounded body back toward us through shoulder-high elephant grass. He was still alive at that point. The searing photo showed a dying Jacques, head torqued downward on a poncho. The photo hit the newsstands before the notification of death to Jacques surviving family. That's how they found out….from an unctuous, front-page of a magazine with a staff obsessed with literary fame.

He was 21 years old.

I have never since bought and always declined to read any of the drivel that drove Newsweek out of business. The editors who published that photo permanently demonstrated they were devoid of class, taste and any semblance of journalism integrity.

At some point thereafter, the first of two NVA pith helmets came into view. I shot and thought I hit the first one to my right. He dropped and I never saw him again and presumed I'd hit him. I didn't care…just wanted him to "go away." But the second moved up one of the many trench lines the NVA dug toward the combat base west of the garbage dump every night before the siege, raised his AK-47 and was about to send my then malnourished, skinny ass to Jesus. I sent him to Buddha first with a lucky shot right "between the running lights." Understand my visual acuity noted in earlier graphs and the fact that I barely qualified as a "Marksman" when I left Camp Lejeune. Shot a191out of 250 a year after after more than half of my Paris Island boot camp platoon went "unq" (unqualified) at the range. The subsequent investigation at Paris Island blamed a boxcar, left parked in the sun too long, with overheated 7.62 ammunition, for the shoddy shooting. Our drill instructors, however, would hear none of it and brought it to our "attention" myriad times thereafter. For Marines, to be "unq" qualifies as him (or her) as "unsat" (unsatisfactory) in Corps parlance, lower than the scales on a snake's belly. And your winter green, formal uniform call "Alphas" made you look naked without the requisite qualification medal. I didn't make "Sharpshooter" until years later as a Reservist. And never shot "Expert," except for the two whose tickets I attempted to punch for Buddha.

I'll bet they thought I was an expert sniper.

There ensued the second bizarre incident. As the extraction team moved back toward the company area, radios still all dead, I encountered Marine Bill Jayne. Bill re-appeared recently on my Facebook page, has retired from Federal civil service as an administrator of the Federal military cemetery system and now lives in North Carolina. On Feb. 25, however, he was part of the first squad in Jacques platoon that attempted to envelop the NVA ambush and that squad suffered the full brunt of the initial volleys. He was coming up one of the many trench lines the NVA nightly dug toward our down our perimeter with a bullet wound in one of his feet. All other eleven members of that squad perished in one burst of fire. The third and final incident of the afternoon, around 1600, occurred when we were retrieving some of the wounded. One of the surviving corpsmen had to be brought back on a stretcher sitting up because a large shell or bullet hole had pierced his right lung and diaphragm.

You could see "through" him as he struggled just to breathe. It was a hole in his thorax the size of a golf ball. I will take that image to my grave. It's part of the reason why I was not prepared for the first 40 minutes of the film "Saving Private Ryan." The imagery therein is brilliant as it replicated combat as real as it gets…..and it bumped me back to 1968. It was a real PTSD throwback. The visual violence was complemented by the sound track. Real noise in combat is hard to replicate. Combat is overpowering loud. That film absolutely captures it.

The pain of day would, nevertheless, linger through another 30 as MACV, then led by Gen. Creighton Abrams, carried the ordered yoke of the infamous Commander-in-Chief (LBJ) to cease all aggressive combat action outside the base perimeter. So there we sat….watching our dead and dying…. ordered to do……nothing.

Several days later, I was ordered off the combat base as I was, at that point, more than 13 months outside of CONUS (Continental United States) and more than a week over the mandatory13-month tour of duty for Navy personnel. This was a peculiarly acute problem for the Marines as the death of several Marines "in country" past their rotation date generated several nasty Congressional inquiries throughout 1967 and 68. So sometime in early March (and I do not remember the specific date), I trudged to the northern end of the flight line with all the combat gear and my sea bag of uniforms and personal clothing…..and waited.

After the afternoon shelling ceased, a C-130 dropped out of the clouds, came full throttle to the end of the runway, pivoted, dropped its ramp and ejected a forklift that began to bounce wildly down the runway's northern end. Although the propeller noise was deafening, the plane's crew chief clearly signaled to "get our asses onboard" as the airplane began its ascent. The engines never decelerated and the plane turned on a quarter and begun the takeoff. For those unfamiliar with the now ancient but reliable transport, it is massive and I felt like a track star coming down the runway, up the ramp and onto the escape bird. Almost immediately the incoming rounds began anew and the 130 did a steep climb that's not in the standard training manual. For those unfamiliar with a 130, think of the rescue plane used in the Hollywood film "Air Force One" for the final stunt scene in the film. At about1500 feet, the craft leveled off with a thump to our cheers and relief. If you've never had the "thrill" of sliding toward the tail ramp of an elevating C-130 at about 200-mph, you missing something Disney can't replicate. The flight to Danang followed with dreams of a hot shower and no incoming.

Two days later a planeload of us Marines, rotating back to "the World," left on a PanAm flight from Okinawa directly to the Marine Corps Air Station at El Toro, CA. Upon debarkation, we picked up our sea bags to go to the transit barracks when this fat-ass, overweight (circa 30-50 lbs.) Sergeant Major came roared onto the tarmac from who knows where screaming:

"Fall in, Marines, just because you're back from the fucking 'Nam doesn't mean you're not still in the fucking Corps!" And this was a senior staff non-commissioned officer who was "bare-chested." He had no ribbons or awards that identified service in Vietnam. His credibility was minimal among the assembled debarking troops, most of us of "grunt" persuasion, and his people skills even less so. He was likely one of the staff NCOs/dinosaurs that the Corps flushed the following decade. About that time, a tall "force recon" sergeant (E-5) stepped forward, bent down toward the Sergeant Major and intoned:

"I'll take this formation, Sergeant Major. You can leave now!" There followed a terse, intense pause as the young sergeant was a lean

6-feet-three –inches or so and had fire in his eyes. The rotund sergeant major declined to press the issue any further. It was a prudent choice on his part. He likely was spared a trip to the El Toro dispensary.

That was the immediate end of my nightmare but not for my brethren in Bravo still back at Khe Sanh. The siege extended until its apogee 30 March when Bravo Company led the breakout. I had a long-time friend whom I helped to bury some years later after a losing bout with Agent Orange-induced prostate cancer, Quilles Ray (Q-Ray) Jacobs. He was with Bravo during the breakout and later awarded a Bronze Star for combat excellence that day. He described in detail in 1981-82 the ferocity and the savagery of the fight that included the last recorded time Marines "fixed bayonets." Q-Ray was part of it and he couldn't tell the story without a plethora of tears. The whole thing was very up close and personal. Bravo caught many of the NVA by surprise arising from their bunkers. Several of them raised their hands in a vain attempt to surrender.

The after action reports that day likely showed no prisoners taken. Bravo wasn't in the mood for it. We wanted "payback."

The final, awful tally of 25 February was 27 KIA out of approximately 45 of us in two platoons. Now commonly called the "Ghost Patrol," the real pain of the month was the visual of Marine bodies rotting in the sun in full view of the company members.......and the order to stand down from recovery. It still grinds veterans of the siege to this day that the corpses were left and ought to remind all American citizens to never commit to a fight that you cannot absolutely win.

The price is too high.

Combine that awful February day with the deaths of Lt. Hank Norman, the Forward Observer with whom I worked, and my radio operator replacement with then Capt. Ken Pipes on March 30 and both my birthdate (Feb. 26) and April 1 have an acrid taste in my mouth every year.

"Semper fi" does not mean leaving your dead and wounded to fester in the open. March, 1968: The taste in my mouth is still rancid.....and this is 2016.

"How Bout 'dem Condom Catheters"

February (2016) marked the ninth anniversary of my introduction to the wonders of the "condom catheter" on a gurney at Scripps Green Medical Center in LaJolla, California. And what, you say, tripped this trip south of my border? Try an 80 percent occlusion of my right, ventricle artery. The term "coronary episode" would be accurate but most people would call it a heart attack.

So this is my concession speech. All Marines, replete with the requisite attitude, must eventually concede that they are no longer six-feet-tall and bullet proof at some point. Patrick adjusted to the reality of five-feet-eight inches and destructible, although I still have the requisite "grunt" attitude: Not as lean but forever as mean. And I am one of those guys who did most things right: Never smoked, kept in decent shape, not obese, paid attention to diet and made it through two wars, Vietnam and the Gulf. But, just like the Plavix commercials, what nailed me was my gene pool appended to that ugly little gremlin cholesterol. As my local cardiologist reminded me: I did most things right but you can't control age or gene pool. It's that toxic mix on both the maternal and paternal side that precipitated the event. All of that circuitously targets the major point of this health homily.

Never be such a hominid imbecile as to go into denial when your ticker tells you that it's out of whack. I was shopping at one of those boring Big Lot stores in Hemet, California the day before my birthday (Feb. 26) in 2007 when I bent over to get something for my daughter. At that point I felt something like a kid's battery-powered toy on my chest. Went immediately home (a retrospectively dumb move) and handed my wife, Anita, the keys and said "We're going to the ER!" I walked into the Hemet (CA) Hospital emergency room and said to the attendant nurse: "I believe I'm having a heart attack."

Her response: "May I see your insurance card?"

My retort: "Did you hear what I just said?" Her facial response only confirmed what she was really thinking. "Oh, God, when the hell is this shift over?" I was having a coronary episode but she suffered from terminal boredom. She practiced rote medicine by presumptive script.

Twenty-four hours later and a $2,700 ambulance ride to Scripps Hospital in San Diego with three women (a driver, paramedic and a nurse), I was on that gurney headed immediately to the operating room. First glance would define the experience as frightening. It was not. I've been more uptight at the dentist getting my teeth capped. And, for the record, I still have my original chompers. I came in with them and I'm leaving with 'em. Say "Amen" to the congregation!

What made the experience less than terrifying was the medical staff at Scripps and their patient protocol. As we exited the ambulance, a nurse from Texas named Kozlewski (no lie!) grabbed my hand, never let it go during the procedure, and then narrated the entire sequence. She enunciated in detail what was about to happen, stayed with me during the process and made the experience almost relaxing, even with my new condom catheter. Believe it or not, I was conscious, but partially sedated, during the entire angioplasty and saw the whole thing on a television monitor poised and tilted to the front ......in living color. To quote a bad '60s cliché: What a trip! Now I have a new body part, a stent that failed in the spring of 2011 and I had to have the same procedure done again at the same spot in my right ventricle artery, except here in Kentucky. But it's not like having a replacement valve for your SUV! Five percent of all stents fail....that's one in 20 for the mathematically challenged. Had the same symptoms, same part of the chest, but a different venue for Angioplasty II. You won't find that caveat in the fine print.

Whom do I sue? An old friend and attorney in Orange, CA delivered the reality check that a lawsuit would have a slim chance of recovery after five years. Recovery is only an option within 365 days. That's the warranty on most body parts. My resident cardiologist here at Lourdes Hospital in Paducah, KY (John Broadbent....and one of the great ones!) assured me that I likely get another 10 to 20 years of life, but no guarantees or warranty.

The two surgeons who did the original procedure went about it as calmly as most of us would change a flat tire. Their subsequent bill confirmed why. Expensive flat tire! It paid for the Mercedes and the BMW. The younger of the two (who appeared to be about 19), I nicknamed "Surfer Dude." At one point during the process, blood spurted from my right thigh (the insertion point for angioplasties) onto the screen poised in front of my face.

"Hey, Surfer Dude," I said. "Either you cut your finger or am I in deep shit" "Naw, "he responded, "We'll just try the other leg." Thankfully I came back from both wars with all body parts appropriately attached. "I don't care which leg you use, just don't go up the middle."

Words fail description as I watched them trail the insertion tube into my heart. Fascinating! As the stent settled in place in the upper quadrant of the artery, I felt more like I was in the middle of a Discovery

Channel episode. The whole operation took less than two hours and, aside from the fact that it was a serious protocol, it was almost relaxing because of the narration, the communication and the good humor of the staff. It almost makes me want to move back to California......... almost, right after Governor Moonbeam and his team of trolls finally quit feeding his career at the public troth. Thus I will now address the crux of today's sermon.

I started regularly seeing a cardiologist when I was 39. Had no specific symptoms of any disease then but I did know that smoking literally killed both of my parents prematurely and I was prone to chronic bronchitis, a condition aggravated by Southern California smog. Yet, despite my pre-emptive precautions, I was tagged. Years ago I did an interview with my then cardiologist published in the weekly for the employees of the Long Beach (CA) Naval Shipyard and he said the three most dangerous substances to heart health were nicotine, cocaine (see comedian Richard Pryor) and onerous levels of caffeine. And caffeine was a very distant, improbable third on that list.

As is obvious since our move here in 2007, Tobacco Road may not be the Interstate 5 but it is alive with traffic in Kentucky. Marry tobacco to chronic obesity, an obsession with pork and fried foods and you have an eventual deadly cocktail of heart-hammering, heart-stopping molecules that will shove your cockpit into instant vapor lock. I have a long-lost friend from New York City who once used to be a heroin junkie. Angelo asserted that kicking the heroin habit took him three weeks. It took 30 years before he finally lifted the albatross of cigarettes. He claims, not without serious, scientific support that nicotine was far more addictive. Subsequent studies confirm Angelo's observation.

You get no argument here.

Preaching "at" people is ineffective, so how do you get a populace on the brink of a diabetes tsunami to be heart healthy? There is no one, simple solution. Forget the ads that promise you instant 72-hour results, including that bizarre, fake cigarettes that expel water currently the "cure" rage. If it were that easy, tobacco wouldn't be one of the economic mainstays of Kentucky agriculture. My less than erudite assessment is that ya'll who want a healthy heart have to have a "Come to Jesus!" moment and that will vary from person to person. Maybe he'll have to get out of the boat, walk on water again and slap you and St. Peter silly on shore. My current motivators are my two children, one with a recently-minted baccalaureate from Thomas More College in Crestview Hills, KY. Adriana has her BA and is now almost 25 while Sean is in the middle pursuit at this juncture at Murray State University. My father was a two-pack a day guy, died when I was 15 and it devastated me for years. With Deitific permission, and my co-operation, I will pile up more years here than either of my parents. He died at 51; she died at 73.

So kick the foul-smelling tobacco habit, lose some weight, lay off the Southern fried and don't do the "denial thing" when you heart delivers a message of distress. Or watch/listen to the Richard Pryor's savagely funny stage rendition of a heart attack a generation ago. He was only 37 when he had his myocardial infarction. How he made fun of a coronary on stage with an audience is pure comedic genius. It's a skit we should force upon all future heart patients. Cardiologists should make it mandatory viewing for those patients with the requisite bad habits cited earlier.

I'll recuse my self from the jury of opinion if my Yankee attitude offends. But I don't think I've said anything that most rational adult readers don't already know. Don't shoot the messenger. Heed the message. And maybe succumb to the seduction that gorgeous Mormon woman hawking Nutri-System preaches. She might save your life. And remember.........

Pork kills; sugar enables.

And, in every form: Tobacco is the undertaker!

Requiescat In Pace

For those of us called to serve, every Memorial Day is sacred reminder what this nation suffered and continues to do so. For veterans scorched by combat, the external scars may heal but the internal fester like third-degree burns. To remember and feel the residual of combat pain is not dysfunctional, but a necessary process of grieving which all Americans should share.

We now have many thousands of Iraqi and Afghani vets grappling with same blisters of emotion suffered from Valley Forge to Gettysburg through the killing fields of Europe and now Southwest Asia. This nation was never quite ready these last 15 years since 9/11 to address the aftermath of so many young warriors returning with horrific injuries. Now is the time to reach out to them, hold on and don't let go. Their combat experiences now define their remaining adult lives, both positively and negatively.

Members of my own family have served in every generation since the Civil War. As previously noted, my great-great grandfather was a member of the 121th Pennsylvania Cavalry at Gettysburg and one of only seven of 121 men in his company who survived Pickett's charge. Also noted within these pages, walking those infamous 1500 meters to the Confederacy high water mark in 1989, emotion overcame where a simple stone marker anchors the point where a Confederate American charged and died nearest the Union lines. You can feel the ghosts among the rocks, howling through both Big and Little Round Tops, swimming through the high grass.

When I wrote the following, it was therapy to assuage a conflicted experience. James Edward Lawrence, USMC died early AM on the morning of December 21 1995. I was awakened by an intense dream during which I found him at the door to my back patio.

Just a dream,right? He appeared like a hologram and we began to converse. "Jim, why are you here?" Then I awoke and looked at the clock. It was 0331. While processing Jim's body at the Los Angles coroner's office two days later, his wife handed me the death certificate. It affixed the time of death precisely through the police report and was the first hint of the timeline of his last moments on earth.

He died at exactly 0330.

James E: A Tribute

H is ice-blue, Irish eyes were lasers of passion. Political conversation brought his hormones to an abject boil. Lame, trite wisdom exchanged over cappuccino or whatever was the vogue white wine made him retch. James E. didn't just observe life, he devoured it. The Irish extremes of passion were his composite elixirs: wine, women and song. He claimed to sing poorly so women and wine took primacy although his rugby cronies might say otherwise.

Four generations later, Celtic-Americans are part of the vulgar culture's easy prey. Name an Irish joke not marinated in liquor. You can't because the stereotype still prevails today. It's now, at this juncture in the morning 1212 hours, 27 December 1995. Check the St. Patrick's Day commercials and memorabilia. Mickey Finn still lives. Revel in the remarkable poetry that the Irish create but always remind the audience that Eugene O'Neil loved whiskey as much as language. Ethnic humor was, however, a peripheral adjunct to Jim. He knew the albatross that we the Irish carry. It's the triple gorillas of alcohol, melancholy and ancillary depression. Although the British take the rap for the Irish genocide, Catholicism for guilt, the Irish in America have never shed the stereotype.

James Edward Lawrence resented that and it fueled his fire as an actor.

How many refugees from the '60s have the "huevos" to chuck a lifestyle we despise and turn the corner on a new choice at age 50? Two tours in Vietnam, one in recon and a second in artillery, cued the indelible slide to self-immolation. James E. returned, went to law school and abruptly trashed a lucrative career he perceived populated by Pharisees and Sadducees. Subsequent years in the mortgage brokerage business confirmed his cynicism and led him to the weathervane that pointed to acting.

I first heard about James E. in Seal Beach, CA from the then Chief of Lifeguards, Timothy John Dorsey, another Irishman of similar party persuasion. He had a friend who could regale you with James E. stories of excess ranging from the exploits of the rugby team to drinking jousts that lasted overnight. One such exploit claimed Jim took his entire ruby team from "The Irisher" in Old Town Seal Beach to LAX (Los Angles International) and flew them all to his hometown of Washington, D. C. on his credit card. Details of the 24-hour party faded into history but the story became legend. The sobriety bill the ensuing day was a good time of more than $5,000. Then at the Belmont Athletic Club in Belmont Shore, Long Beach in 1983, I met James E. No doubt who he was! Witness the gold "jump" wings tattooed on his chest, a proud relic of his time in the lst Force Reconnaissance Battalion. I heard about the tattoo years before so the legend morphed into reality in the Club's Jacuzzi.

"You're James Edward Lawrence," I said. "Your reputation doth precede you."

Thus began an enduring friendship that ushered both of back to the U. S. Marine Corps Reserve. That of which he was most overtly proud was the fit into his boot camp "dress greens," the uniform of the day Marines call "Alphas." He first earned them at age 20. How many 50-year-old Marines can so brag?

Lean and mean, even until death.

Had he not dropped that affiliation with the reserves in 1993, maybe the slide might have stopped. The fraternity of U. S. Marines is group therapy. Those of you who perceive the Corps as a footnote to paleontology have no clue. Marines are warriors, not "knuckle-draggers." Go to the field with "03 walk-a-lots" (infantry) or "gun grunts" (artillery) for a stint of active duty and you will see motivation rarely found in the civilian sector. James E. was the penultimate Marine, a staff sergeant who excelled more than most Marine officers, a class of people he found self-absorbed in their circle of career. Twenty-seven years after his last Vietnam patrol, James E. walked into the ambush of alienation, anger, alcohol and depression. That's a ton of firepower to fight. Jim could bring "steel on target" as a forward observer and chief of the "fire direction control center." But the final ambush was starkly simple.

James Edward Lawrence swallowed the barrel of his M-19, .45-caliber pistol with one round chambered in front of actress Virginia Massey, the paramour with whom passion re-awoke. She decided to quell the affair; he decided to quell his life. The summer of his years ended on the first day of winter, 1995. Like radioactive fallout, myriad lives about him swallowed the spillover violence. Suicide is never solitary. It's a final burst of anger, like ripples in a pond that disrupt all attached to the deceased. I have a gaping whole in my soul that I doubt time will ever fill and only those who walked Quang Tri Province or the sands of Anbar Province can ever completely understand. Marines connect in a mystical bond of brotherhood that is monastic in depth, akin to the rule of St. Benedict. Those bonds never cease with death.

The last time we had dinner together was at the Denny's near Sunet Boulevard and Gardener Avenue in Hollywood, one of LA's great behavioral sinks. It's a Mecca for hookers, mavens, rock icons and "transitionals" on the downward slide of life. Don Henley may have had it in mind when he wrote "Sunset Grill."

One block away was the studio apartment that was home to his scripts, books and thespian aspirations. Sixty minutes to the south were his wife and four sons. It was never a dichotomy with which he was completely at ease. The acting passion was an intoxication about to become a gig with more than just applause, one that actually paid money. No one, however, ever painted Jim as a paradigm of patience. His apartment was a meticulous blend of Catholic, Irish and Marine. But Jim also embraced that "Black Irish Heart," the proclivity toward the tragic, passion without fruition, soul wandering aimlessly.

James E. was first wounded in 1968. Yet his 27-year MEDEVAC chopper never made it to the battalion aid station. America may think the Wall has reached its quota, all casualties counted, all dead listed by name.

Not true.

Add James Edward Lawrence to the black granite wall. Our "wounded in action".......and "after-action" continue to die. Like Jim's four sons, the decedent's survivors will ask: Why? Unlike some of Jim's harlequin peers of the theater, there are no answers. James E. no longer inhabits our world.

Requiescat in pace! May his soul, and all the souls of the faithful departed, rest in peace. Amen!

And Semper fi!

Post Traumatic Dreams

The in-vogue phrase "post-traumatic stress syndrome" morphed into trite panoply of behaviors mental health scions can't seem to meld into a coherent definition. Vietnam through Afghanistan stoked that blaze. Yet it is a normal digression of the cerebral swerve to our animal self in the face of terminal threat to life. Thus Post Traumatic Stress Syndrome (PTSD) is confirmation of our bifurcated struggle between biology and the rational mind that percolates to the surface under the intense stress pre, peri and post combat. Now in 2016, it's just called PTS. We've dumped the "drome" part.

St. Thomas Aquinas correctly identified the conflict polarity as the struggle between "ens rationale" (rational being) and "ens biologis" (biological being). They are complementary poles of the same human personality. Together they make up the overarching "ENS" (caps mine) that includes both the human biology or body and the mind or rational thought process. In healthy people, the two are in balance.

In combat they are not. Combat permanently corrupts that balance for a lifetime.

It re-verts your entire "ens" (that which defines you as a unique creature) toward the biological animal whose primal instinct must be self-preservation…..at any cost. Thus it is the thrust that drives you to co-hese with your combat fraternity to the exclusion of all else much as a pack of wolves or pride of lions would react to a group threat. But the process shift to the biological accelerates at warp speed.

When faced with a threat to life in combat or individually, your body transforms suddenly and violently. Your vision and blood pressure instantly accelerate and become more acute along with your hearing. All bodily apertures slam shut after an adrenaline rush that signals the call to launch unison action. It tells you "this is not the time for a head call." You hyperventilate to rush the stream of adrenaline and secondary ammunition of sugar throughout your system. The mission of survival becomes paramount. Destruction of the threat, or the enemy posing it, moves your "ens rationale" to the bench. Love thy neighbor, ISIS or otherwise, is not on the agenda. The alarm cedes to biology and assumes command.

When I first posed this description to a medical doctor while I was in undergraduate school, she thought the description was too suspect with simplicity....but she listened. Most combat veterans, however, would concur. You don't fight for "mom, apple pie, the flag" and all that patriotic drivel. Your primary concern is the warriors with whom you stand, their survival and the triumph of the group over the adversary. If necessary, you must be willing to cede your own life......as thousands have....for the band of brothers and sisters to your left and right.

Yet what combatants rarely predict and confront poorly is the aftermath. And it is also part of the reason they return for "multiple tours of duty" to battle milieus that mimic more logic to them than the plastic illusion of peace at home. One minute you're fighting for your life and days later you're "back in the hood" with friends and relatives who have limited sense of your trauma.

Extended combat is so intense that the "problem" becomes the peace that ensues when you leave the "kill zone" and the warrior group with whom you bonded more closely than marriage. The emotion of spending extended periods of high stress generates a kind of motif riddled with guilt or depression. So it poses the question: Why did I survive? I feel badly about it but don't know why. Why did they die and I survived?

Thus warriors begin the slow trek back from the war zone to the mundane, droll ritual of everyday life. That's the seed packet of PTSD when you attempt to re-integrate into society that seems to be afoul, asunder and different from the one you left. Your vision of what was skews the new reality of what is.

That intensity and commitment are rarely replicated in civilian life. As an adrenaline rush, not even sex surpasses the focus of combat. It is an all-consuming physical and emotional experience.

Society hasn't changed much. You have! It seems static but you will never be the same. You're not insane but you know somehow "you don't completely fit." Your center of gravity shifted and constricted. It's another clichéd fork in the road. The warrior's choice can either elevate or devolve. The vast majority of sustained trauma victims and combatants return to stasis and balance. Much like a boat buffeted by high seas that returns to calm water, we re-integrate. Real survivors of combat grow from it.

But the cerebral creep of post-traumatic stress begins with the subconscious and the dreams thereafter. What counselors, psychiatrists and psychologists call "flashbacks" is a nebulous term that encompasses a spectrum of memories, both real and imagined for those afflicted by the trauma of combat, rape or ongoing emotional assault. It is a category of experience almost too vague to apply to everyone with the same empirical jargon. Now we live with the phrase "intrusive memory." What was stamped onto the plate of one's memory is morally neutral……but it's there. Combat trauma is not like a broken radiator you can return to Wal-Mart. No warranty and no refund! At that point the combat "experience" is part of what defines you and your "ens." Grapple with it and incorporate it in some positive way. The other choice is to endow it as a negative anchor to the rest of your life.

When I returned from the Tet Offensive in Vietnam (1968), it was six years before I had such deceleration into the emotional pit. I was 29 and then living with a girlfriend who took me home to her place after a bicycle collision with a truck broke my jaw. One night I dreamed that I was back at Khe Sanh trying to call an artillery strike in the perimeter trench line "behind the wire" when the North Vietnamese came storming over and my M-16 jammed. I turned the rifle around and used the butt plate to hit one of the oncoming NVA in the face, screaming loudly when I rolled over, hit her in the head and jolted her awake…… and out of bed. I then sat up and began calling in the artillery strike. That was a PTSD devolution.

But here's the truth: That NEVER happened in real life!

It was purely a composite figment of my imagination but I can attest that it scared both of us. So was it a "flashback" or just an ordinary nightmare? You judge.

As I got older, strange combat dreams like that became more frequent and common, including very vivid ones where I was deployed to Iraq, Kosovo and Afghanistan. Again…and for the record: I served in Vietnam and the Gulf War but left the Marine Corps in 2000, all before those latter conflicts ensued. So what generated those dreams? Images from the nightly news? Films? A current VA psychologist here in Kentucky told me that PTSD does NOT diminish with age but ignites a relentless rerun like waves onto a beach like bad old movies you are forced to see again.

It helps to cope with the night messages but never inoculates the mind from their intrusions. Sleep post combat is often furtive and too often elusive. Understand the syndrome, admit its presence. Confront and neutralize it. It's 2016 and I'm still on a four-hour sleep cycle, just like standing watch in Vietnam. So don't give me this tripe that PTS recedes with age.

It's 0328 as I write this.

But never let it control that sacred balance between biology and the mind and, most importantly, your soul.

The Force(d) March of Life: Family

Had you said in 1965 that my peripatetic romp through life would include a homestead in Kentucky via California, you would invite a blistering array of sarcasm and laughter. Be apprised that I grew up in an Irish-Catholic family.....and I need no grief about my English surname.

Somebody in my gene pool literally slept with the enemy.

My branch of the Fitch family may have started near the Whales-England countryside but, like a lot of Irish and sideways English criminal types, a trip to Ireland or Australia/New Zealand sure seemed a better choice than a British jail. My mother was legitimately Irish by ancestry as she was a Coyne (shortened from the O'Coyne) and her mother a McGrail. As she often intoned to me and harangued my Father, there were only three mantras for the Irish to follow: "Drop the 'O,' loose the broagh and get a job!" Ruth Frances Coyne was born in 1911 and her mother died in childbirth, an omen of things to come for her first two children who also died in infancy. Her father was a big Irish Pittsburgh cop named Thomas Patrick Coyne. His picture adorns the hallway of our house and has for the duration of our marriage. He died during her senior year of high school at St. Mary's of the Mount

High School in Pittsburgh. She had no siblings.

Ruth Frances was a child classical piano prodigy who had her own organ duet show with a partner on Sunday nights on KDKA radio in Pittsburgh right after high school, a career she abandoned to marry my father, Charles Eugene in 1936. Only after her death did my sister and I discover why the "good Catholic" girl married in the parish rectory rather than with a nuptial Mass in the parish church.

Que pasa?

She was pregnant with my older brother, Charles.

Baby was on time. Marriage was late. Virginity was much more in vogue then and the shame attached to pre-marital sex was very alive in 1936, a stark contrast to today that wouldn't even evoke a yawn or a ripple in church. Women eight months pregnant walk up the aisle in Virgin white and no one blinks. Shortly after my older brother, Charles, died during the St. Patrick's day floods of 1937, thereafter my older sister, Rosemary, arrived. Both died before I was born. Why and how were not questions that either one of my parents would answer. When I once broached the question of how, my mother's answer: "It's none of your business!" In mid-life my sister and I went on a search for their graves and found them, buried together, in a vertical tandem plot at Resurrection Cemetery in Pittsburgh on a hill overlooking the Monongahela River. The plot has no headstones and they lay without any markers. The cemetery records showed they apparently died of SIDS (Sudden Infant Death Syndrome). They were both less than a year old. My parents then had no money for a "proper burial" as it was the height of the Great Depression.

My father, Charles Eugene, drifted through a series of jobs, scored a year of undergraduate school at Duquesne University and, sometime during the first Roosevelt administration, became virulently anti-FDR.

He had one of the few jobs still necessary during the Great Depression for Duquesne Light Co., the utility that serviced most of Western Pennsylvania. His job was to shut off the electricity of the many for whom payment of their electric bills was a choice: Power or food.

It was during of these shutoff notices that he arrived at a local hog farmer's home as he was destroying more than 250 of his pigs. The collapse of the hog market and policies of the Federal Department of Agriculture did not generate sufficient market price/income for him to maintain the numbers. So, as my dad recanted, he watched the farmer herd the animals into a large pit, shoot them and bury them. To his dying day he was livid about farm policies that destroyed food supplies as the bulk of his then workday addressed the issue on a real human basis. The intent of the New Deal administration was to stabilize hog prices but destruction of food when others were starving completely offended and perplexed my father.

Hell of a choice...........food or lights!

That's when he became a lifelong Republican with a thorough distaste for Roosevelt. He did, however, actively root for John F. Kennedy's inclusion onto the Democratic Party national ticket in 1956. When Adlai Stevensen chose Estes Kefauver from Tennessee as his running mate, my dad saw the choice as further evidence of anti-Catholic bias throughout America. The subtle seepage of that bigotry still exists even today in the "New South."

The watershed shift, however, for both my parents and an entire generation occurred at 0743, Dec. 7, 1941. My dad was drafted shortly thereafter into the U. S. Navy at age 31and spent the next four years on active duty until 1945. Somewhere among his memorabilia was his draft notice that read "for the duration of the war and six months thereafter." Few contemporary Americans can even conceive of that. The

original estimates of the duration of World War II were 7-10 years...
.well into the 1950s.

That changed the whole equation for my father, my father-in-law and roughly 16 million members of the expanded American military in service at the time. Father in the Atlantic on a destroyer; father-in-law (Joe Rodriguez) on an aircraft carrier in the Pacific.

Both left active service as Second Class Petty Officers (E-5). They were part of Tom Brokaw's "Greatest Generation" because they had to be. Argue you may about the impact of Hiroshima and Nagaski and its adjunct horror in 1945 but it gets minimal traction from the surviving remaining members of the U. S. populace that lived through World War II. To them, Hitler and Tojo represented real evil in the world and had to be destroyed. Delenda est Carthago! Carthage must be destroyed. The Romans did it all so thoroughly that their final insult was to salt the enemy agricultural fields to preclude recovery.

"Sympathy for the devil(s)" was not a tune my father and father-in-law sang.

At the end of the war in '45, my dad's Navy career ended but not after he declined an officer's commission with the Navy Seebees. His previous job history in construction and his innate intelligence obviously impressed some in the chain of command but he didn't want to be a Navy Ensign at age 35. When I once asked him why he didn't take it, he demurred with typical "Charley" humor with "I don't want to land on some god-forsaken island with a Tommy gun in one hand and a shovel in the other." But it then took more than a decade for him to regain a foothold in the building industry as a supervisor of construction for the U. S. Army Corps of Engineers. The armories in Butler, PA, Wheeling, West Va. and Cadiz, OH are three stops on his Army Corps of Engineers resume intertwined with stints on both the Monongahela and Alleghany Rivers. His cherished, final posting was the construction of Pike Island Dam on the Ohio River just north of Wheeling, West VA. But his premature death at age 51, at the acme of his Federal career, short-changed the family because, at that time, you needed five years of Federal service to qualify for a pension. He died with four years and 11 months of Federal Civil Service that essentially locked us into an enduring cycle of poverty. My mother got not even a "thank you every so much" from the Feds.

Thus she raised two teens almost exclusively on Social Security that I remember was a mere $220/month and $35 per month from a small U. S. Navy service check. She was eligible for "the dole," as she called it (Welfare Assistance), but too proud to take it and took her refusal steadfastly to the grave with her in 1983. Although that frustrated both my sister and me, she never wavered about that choice.

"I will never accept a handout!" still rings in my head today. It was one of my early lessons in life. There is no greater reality in a lifetime of harsh realities and, no, God goes not dish out equal hands in the timeline of life. It's how you play that hand that defines you, your legacy and eventual success.

Things to Like About Kentucky

Since the internet bludgeons us all with sundry lists from mundane to morose, allow an incursion into that swamp with some of my own. Of the many irritating traits this commonwealth adopted since its admission to the union, there is a contrasting number of little things to relish consistent with its eclectic culture. I listed them in no order of precedence but they stand in contrast to places (e.g. New York and LA) fraught with urban decay where the human stampede tramples peace and reflection.

- The rural mail carriers here straddle the drive shaft of their own automobiles, steer with their left hands and sort the mail with their right. Although disconcerting at first glance, it's standard practice. And, no, it's not distracted driving! Over the years, conversation with our mail carrier revealed that the U. S. Postal service, among other things, will not reimburse rural carriers if they elect to modify their vehicles so the steering column is on the right side. "Dummy me" thought it would be a safety issue for the USPS but they provide the carriers with amber warning lights, carrier flags and bumper attachments that identify them as USPS. That apparently suffices. "Mary Doughty, our route

Mail Lady," provides real "service" we never saw in California where she actually drives up to our house (c. 200 meters from the front road) when necessary and delivers any package to the safety of the alcove that protects the front door. Unlike urban elsewhere, she doesn't just leave that perfunctory little pink notice to "pick it up" at the nearest Post Office more than seven miles from here. She also checks any outgoing mail for correct postage so you won't have necessary items summarily returned. This month the owner/operator (that would be me) forgot to put a stamp on the monthly missive to those marvelous, notoriously competent folks at Chase Mortgage for whom I have less than unbridled, unbinding affection. She checked it and left it with the incoming so I could correct the error that day. When I often see her on the road, we actually converse. She knows about our kids, our past history and likely a lot of our private life since she's privy to our bills. Urban life is immunized from that kind of human touch and her charm provided a new perspective on the U. S. Postal Service that most of us think has no face. She epitomizes civility and common courtesy. Her service thus reminds us of what we lost in the urban/suburban sprawl of most of 'modern" America that tramples on the human touch of business. Although Mary's brand of public relations may disappear within the next generation, it is today something to savor. With the upcoming demise of Saturday deliveries, the likely next step for many will be a centralized mail substation or series of said to which the mail recipient must transit. It's not a big deal if the collection mailbox is 30 to 50 yards away "down the street" from your home. Consider, however, the change to those of us in rural America, maybe miles from our designated mail reception center, particularly in inclement weather. Mary likely presides over the passing of an era my children's children will never see. When the USPS's public persona has no "personal face to the public," that necessary public support will wane to near zero. The business decision to cede the bulk of Saturday deliveries to either United Parcel Service or FedEx may be the product of current fiscal necessity but it reflects a long-term myopia that aggravates the very problem it intends to mollify. As of this writing, the decision to raise postal rates to $.49 per first-class letter is further confirmation of an alleged "independent" Federal department with as many bosses/overseers/supervisors as employees. The trite old cliché "Too many cooks spoil the broth" here applies. While the USPS writhes to survive, FedEx and UPS lick their chops. Why not raise the letter rate to $1.00 per and be done with it for ten years? Just a suggestion.

• God assigned us an aviary Marine guard for our property: Oliver the Owl. He's about 18-inches tall and generally arrives at dusk and stays throughout the night. Like a sentry at a foreign embassy, Oliver never misses a formation and always shows up for guard detail about 1900, beginning in the spring and throughout the summer. I once got within 30 yards of him for a photograph. Despite our need to decapitate more than 10 large red oaks that threatened our house after the trauma of the 2009 Ice Storm, fear not for his habitat loss. Kentucky has enough trees to supply toilet paper for the nation until Saudi Arabia runs out of oil around 2035. We cheer his nocturnal visits as snakes adorn his favorite dinner menu and we have an adequate share of the non-venomous and a village of Copperheads near the highway viaduct on the western end of the property. And don't berate me with that old, tired bromide about the place "copperheads" have as part of nature's wondrous ecology. There is a reason they acquired the nomenclature. That breed is the cold-blooded semi-Satan that reigns as the model for Act 1 of the Biblical opera cited at the Garden of Eden. Although herpetology is not my strong suite, copperheads secured a reputation in U. S. History with the "Don't Tread on Me!" generated during the Revolutionary War. Their behavior reflects the ideals in the flag and their nasty behavior is well earned. They are 2-3 feet of quiet, deadly dual dentures generally aroused only when cornered or upon which they incur the foot of a larger creature. Most of the time, they'll run at the first sign of intrusion, much like most snakes of the Al Qaida variety. You might not die from a copperhead strike, unlike that of a large Eastern Diamondback Rattlesnake, but the injuries are serious. The year we moved here, a young girl (c. 14-years-old) in a neighboring county suffered an arm bite and lost it by amputation from the elbow down. Thus copperheads are a serious threat of which to be wary but not normally a death sentence. But that's why Oliver is like an insurance policy with a cheap premium. As cited previously, it's only about 2.5 acres but, with three years of tree and brush clearance, we have yet to completely eliminate the persistent honeysuckle vines so favored as cover by anything that crawls. One of the remarkable red oak trees seriously bent and destroyed during the 2009 ice storm was Oliver's dining table where he would take his prey and have a meal. That's where I got the photograph. Now that the tree is gone, he's had to move the dining venue to a couple of large sycamores. Other birds in the sycamore condominium faced forced eviction. Nobody in the local aviary messes with Oliver, not even the hawks or the turkey vultures. The bird epitomizes Robert DeNiro's most famous line from the film "Taxi Driver." "You lookin' at me" Oliver stares, "You must be lookin' at me!" And when he directs that piercing gaze your way........he never blinks. And when he's finally done with your visual intrusion, he just turns away. It's almost like he's saying: "Get outta here, I'm done with you, human!"

- Then there are the world's perfect neighbors: Terrell & Stephanie Mathis. When I first moved to Kentucky, I would pronounce his name as Ter-RELL (emphasis second syllable). It took almost a year here before I heard the preferred pronunciation as TER-rell from his wife. Terrell and Stephanie are both an example of what is best about a neighbor with support, courtesy and the humor of a real gentleman. After retirement from the now shuttered General Tire plant in nearby Graves County after 37 years, Terrell built his custom, retirement home on the west side of the pond that we share. He is super-hero to two of his many grandchildren, victims of the multiple marriage syndrome so prevalent in this part of the world. That is not a cheap side shot on the nuances of Kentucky family life. It is an unfortunate reality. The majority of Kentuckians "west of the Lakes", as the local label portends, marry young and divorce early. As in all separations, the offspring always suffer the most. The Mathis grandchildren are fortunate to have them as their de facto parents because they now fill a void that heals the asunder gap between their birthing parents. My own paternal grandparents lived within 15 minutes walking distance from me in Pittsburgh, PA. Yet I only saw them 2-3 times a year and at Christmas when my dad's father would drive his classic 1937 sedan to our ram-shackled house (with no hot, running water) and give me and my sister a $20-dollar bill. I was almost 30 years old before I encountered peers who actually had a relationship with grandparents. The Mathises are the prototype of what grand-parenting ought to be and articulate the best of what that designation means.

- Finally….the quiet! Those of you who may read this from patches of America's urban sprawl, note the memory of what real silence is. After 30 years in the 5th gear noise chute of Southern California, it is just a daily treat to breathe the still of rural American air. Yes, automobiles do sometimes intrude but the clatter you assume to be a necessary part of life in SoCal is absent here. Night time here beckons me often. I sit on the back (or front) decks of our home and contemplate life "in the stillness," particularly on clear nights with the stars. Scorpio, Aquarius and the Big Dipper are close enough to almost touch in this latitude and they tell you not to allow your ego and vanity to run rampant. It's a humble place to live. Last year I returned to SoCal for what I thought would be a visit to reconnect. Just the opposite happened. The 405 (San Diego) Freeway starkly reminds any visitor that California is the twin victim of both air and noise pollution. You must travel to the high desert above Palm Springs to actually be free from the intrusion of the internal combustion engine. It's a reminder of the necessary interludes we all need as humans. Even the most addicted urbanites from Manhattan need a connection to what is normal and mundane here. Go to the noise.......then drive away!

There are obviously many places on this planet that can so replicate the above. Kentucky is not the only place where said peace exists but it's a helluva lot better choice than the sprawl of Santa Ana to Riverside.

The Distance from
the Bible Belt to the Liquor Store

Much of what defines the commonwealth of Kentucky pivots upon profoundly comic contradiction. There are 120 counties here. Fifty are wet; 70 are dry. Can you say "group schizophrenia"?

Yes, this is still part of the "Bible Belt" where McCracken County in the Confederate west is "wet." Take notice, however, that there is a thriving "moonshine" industry in the dry counties around McCracken that defies extinction and roils in the face of alcohol hypocrisy. Forget the fact that Kentucky has multiple bourbon distilleries, racetracks and a booming marijuana industry adjacent to the West Virginia border where state police and the Federal warriors of Alcohol Tobacco & Firearms often decline to tread. Kentucky leads the nation in at least one industry: Whack Weed! Those who live near the verdant fields of Humboldt, Ca, take heed. You have competition here in the east.

Yet the Kentucky obsession with alcohol suppression persists in the Sunday AM time slot where the outlaw legacy stokes the embers of Prohibition and the festering array of "sneak Baptist" drinkers. Anecdotes here abound about how every family has an "Uncle" who could hide bottles of bourbon throughout the homestead, house or farm. There is an oft recurrent joke here told often how you can recognize the "closet drinkers" at the liquor store. They don't acknowledge one another, nor make eye contact and decline to greet each other, even the clerk who takes their money and who may attend the Sunday AM service along with them at the local, chosen church of choice. And just what did Jesus say about hypocrisy?

"Where's my bullwhip?"

Post Prohibition in 1933, the commonwealth ceded control of alcohol sales to local voting precincts within Kentucky counties. So Mc-Cracken surrounding Paducah eventually voted to be mostly "wet" with the then incorporated City of Lone Oak opting to remain dry. Graves County to the south is now "moist" and Ballard County to west is "dry." What's the distinction, you ask? You are "moist" only when you allow or restrict alcohol sales to a specific voting precinct or business......like a Mexican restaurant that wouldn't be one if not for an attached cantina that serves Margaritas. This is the stuff on which late-night comedy salivates. Incongruity invites laughter and Kentucky has more than its allocated share. Still "My Old Kentucky Home" flies under the sarcasm radar as one of the indigent "forget-about-it, flyover" states. Go to Jefferson County (Louisville), however, where Sunday alcohol sales are legal and the population much more liberal, mainline Protestant and Catholic. As a Josephite priest I know once bellowed during a Sunday sermon: "Catholics are not hypocrites. What do you think Jesus and the apostles did with that wine at the Last Supper?"

Heavy "Duh" factor in play here.

Need we point to the obvious that Jesus and the 12 Apostles (Judas included) drank the wine prior to the subsequent Crucifixion. And, to cite another piece of Biblical history not a parable: Did Jesus change that water to vinegar at the wedding feast of Canaan? Or was that not His first documented miracle? I believe that the wedding host, father of the bride, "saved the best wine until last." Or is that one part of Biblical history where some Christians suddenly acquire amnesia? Residents of this commonwealth hyperventilate about the evils of John Barleycorn but the twin addictions to sugar (and all its manifestations) and pork hardly qualify as sins. More to the point, they don't even come up on the radar. But check the obesity index in Kentucky. Gluttony permeates all tiers of the state from the moonshine crowd to the Mint Julep mamas with $300 bonnets in a size 22 dresses on parade at the track on Derby Day.

We're Number 3, trailing only Alabama and Mississippi in the National Fat (Body) League. Adipose tissue galore, we will make the playoffs in the National Mortality Bowel with a line-up buttressed (pun intended) by obesity, diabetes and coronary occlusions! Hey we're Number Three! If you ain't at least 40 pounds over playing weight, you don't make the varsity. And Kentucky is several tons over playing weight, surpassing most of the rest of the country. Just check the pork patrols at the local morning diners and evening saloons. Think this is hyperbole? Then check with the very large cardiac units at Lourdes and Baptist Health hospitals ten minutes away from this locale and others throughout the state. Pork and obesity keep them in business.

If you haven't yet seen it, rent a copy of the movie "Elizabethtown" (E-Town for you out-of-towners). The film's most endearing feature is how well it captured the human quality and de-amplified, real pace of Kentucky social life. Unlike "Life in the Fast Lane" of Los Angeles, New York and Chicago, locals here actually relish conversation, sometimes to the point of annoyance. You may remember that as an exchange where both parties actually talked "with," rather than "at" each other. What poses as "conversation" in the aforementioned is really: "Please shut up and finish talking so I can tell you what you really need to think!" Strangers here will engage you about anything from the weather to University of Kentucky athletics. At times you must terminate said exchanges with phony excuses just to escape. Kentuckians actually initiate conversation with perfect strangers........ Whether you want it or not! What a concept! As our first attorney here in Paducah, Amy McReynolds, noted eight years ago (and she is from Chicago), there a very different focus where there are no professional sports teams that devour the sports page. "UK" is the hub of the wheel. And University of Kentucky basketball is the crown jewel.

Here in the South, the pre-meal grace is long and tedious as are the served portions that are "muy" abundant. Now let's saunter over to the dinner table and eat! Bourbon may be anathema to these latter-day Carrie Nations but so are Weight Watchers, Nutri-system, TOPS (Take-Off-Pounds-Sensibly) and Jenny Craig. Just ask Paula Deen! Fill that plate and pack that waistline. After all, "ain't hog heavenly"? And how often have you heard this after the blessing of the meal: ""Bless you heart, 'darlin,' ain't this pork just divine!"

You can add more lanes to the San Diego Freeway but that only attracts more traffic and suppression of dialogue. In Southern California, talk radio fills that void. Commuters don't need people....they have a swashbuckling array of AM radio motor-mouths to fill the conversation void. That makes Kentucky a refreshing change from the urban caldron of clatter / chatter of the commute throughout the Golden State, their "nut-job" governor and his obsession with a "bullet train" from Bakersfield to Fresno. After all, doesn't everyone in the tarnished Golden State want to visit Merle Haggard's home?

And, yes, country fans. Nashville may be the country music Vatican but both types of music (country and western) thrive in California. And Haggard did live near Bakersfield but did this year at his home in Redding, CA.

This commonwealth, however, also has its own brand of xenophobia. New arrivals must filter through a screen of intolerance that percolates to the surface in odd places. Exempli gratia: When I first arrived here in the summer of 2007, consider the quirky conversation I had with a clerk at the Lone Oak "Super Valu Grocery Store," she of "big hair" and a mouthful of chewing gum. It's rather obvious from my speech patterns that I'm not from the South. Yankees are like that. We just don't have that beautiful Southern lilt. For the record, I'm from the 'Burgh...... Pittsburgh, as in Pittsburgh Steelers! And I don't even like Kentucky winters, much less those in Western Pennsylvania. California may have parched-baked Septembers, but Pennsylvania has January and February under the influence of the evil Lake Erie. At least it ain't Cleveland, which is one winter's step below Buffalo, Detroit, Chicago and Green Bay.

By the way, "Super Value" is a true oxymoron! It changed its name recently to Banks but, as Jack Webb said years ago on the series "Dragnet": "The name(s) have been changed to protect the innocent."

As the groceries underwent their perfunctory scan, she queried: "What 'church' ya'll belong to?" Sensing a baited question poised for an ambush, I opted for deflection. I wanted not to resurrect a Tennessee Williams, existential dialogue because she informed me the store did not then carry beer in stock. After all, this ain't the wild west of California. The little Satan on my left shoulder prevailed, however, over the Angel on my right. Lord, forgive me for my subsequent inspiration, although it was only a venial sin!

"Kurt Vonnegut's church!"

"What church is that?" she pursued.

"The Cosmic Church of the Utterly Indifferent!"

The ensuing pause was a pregnant silence too dripping with cynicism. Grocery receipt: $17.95; the exchange: "priceless."

Not only are Kentuckians a remarkable mix but the physical beauty of the commonwealth is spiritually enervating. Red and white oak trees abound, wildlife is abundant and the local Wal-Marts sport hunting/fishing sections that could arm a Marine Corps infantry battalion, replete with sufficient camouflage to blind a herd of elk and a platoon of wild turkeys. The truly wooded areas, not yet cleared for housing or agriculture, really have a Daniel Boone quality. Kentucky underbrush defines the word thicket that hosts the full spectrum of animal protein. Since modern America decimated almost all big cat predators, what Kentucky and other Eastern states now confront, is a "deer and coyote problem." Most roads outside of the metropolitan areas of Louisville, Lexington and the Interstates are dual lane. Nocturnal driving has sometimes tragic consequence for both man and animal. Hit a deer at "double-nickel" and both you and the deer inherit a major medical problem. Most of the time, the deer loses along with the vehicle. That's part of the sometimes deadly attraction where nature intersects with people. A local body shop of renown in Draffenville, KY in adjacent Marshall County made a small fortune during the 2010 deer season. They had more than 400 wrecks to fix but the shop owner told me that the insurance companies were livid with the state's failure to extend the hunting season. Kentucky game officials admit a chronic need to control deer overpopulation, then estimated at more than 280,000 head. They also admit hunters need to cull the herd but charge outlandish license fees that discourage the very hunters needed to quell the population. Thus hunters either decline to hunt, ignore the license (at this point, I'm told is $80 per tag with a limit of two deer per season) and take their chances with the game wardens. Marry that to the encroaching destruction of cattle and sheep by coyotes, and behold the combustible brew of cultures that's underway between farmers, hunters and the People for the Ethical Treatment of Animals, vegans all, who will get a rude welcome in an economy built on agriculture. The soil here is rich with corn, tobacco, soybeans, tomatoes and grasses that feed some of the finest Black Angus this side of Montana.

But deer also find corn yummy along with soybeans, garden staples also favored by Poe's favorite ravens, not the Baltimore types. And coyotes will prey on anything from your house cat to raccoons, opossums, squirrels and small deer. That makes it a stand-off between farmer, hunter and nature.

Then, for those who blew off the Tennessee Valley Authority segment in high school U. S. History, behold Kentucky Lake! With a shoreline longer than Lake Michigan, it begins just east of Paducah and extends southward into Tennessee. You can actually sail from the Gulf of Mexico, north through the Mississippi River onto the Ohio, then veer south into the Tennessee River through the lakes all the way to Alabama. The lake has a dual nomenclature, Lake Barkley on the west and Kentucky Lake on the east with a man-made Federal island called the Land between the Lakes (LBL) at the center. It is one of the defining legacies of the Franklin D. Roosevelt administration and the enormous impact the project had on rural electrification. Our home here is a direct by-product of that marvel that embodied the best of what government could do and what it seems grossly unable to perform since the Johnson administration. It will likely never happen again. For those who think there is no intelligent life east of the Colorado River or west of the Hudson, this is one of the country's best-kept secrets. Fish caught in this man-made wonder bring fishermen to Nirvana. The dams on both the northern ends of the two lakes enrich this region and country almost beyond belief. Like similar areas throughout North America, the slow infestation of "real estate" vultures hastened the process of defiling what was once pristine. Don't ignore the dripping sarcasm. It's fully intended. To once again cite Eagle musician Don Henley: "Call someplace paradise………….. Kiss it good-bye!"

So the inherent patina of stranger distrust that permeates local attitude has an unfortunate root in "dollared" reality. Best I can ascertain is God's creation quota of new real estate is over, so the Lakes' shorelines throughout Western Kentucky are up for grabs. Wish it wasn't so! Last time I checked, Avarice (greed for you Rednecks!) was still one of the seven capital sins.

Kentucky is not immune.

The Penultimate High School

If you are a standard American family, you have parents who work 8-10 hours per day, sometimes longer, to buoy the family income. They then parcel "off- duty" time in segments sometimes too short to recharge their emotional batteries. So how do their children exit their work day at 2:30 p.m. and expect to harvest the wealth of a lifetime? Simply put: How does a 30-hour school week prepare students for an eventual lifetime of success?

It doesn't. The Japanese, Indians and Chinese know this. But Americans are still tied to the yoke of a 19th-century school calendar that even John Dewey would now render obsolete. So what's the problem here?

The traditional five-day, nine-month school week with maximized summer "vacations" is a relic of an agrarian 19th century where children worked farms with their families during the "growing season" (May to September). That over-arch then relegated formal schooling to the off-months of fall, winter and early spring. What we have now is a post-modern, global economy where the best educated percolate to the top of the pyramid and the king of the food chain is he or she best educated from language through math and science. That's a code Asian educators long ago deciphered. Those with the most intellectual skill control not only the world economy but every product, idea, insight and novel inventory that business gestates. To punctuate the point, what is the second- largest, English-speaking country in the world? Would you guess the Australia? Canada? Great Britain?

Answer: China with more than 250 million English-speaking citizens. Digest that for a moment.

So, if the number of "geniuses" or innovators like Steve Jobs, Bill Gates or personalities like Oprah Winfrey, writers like Tom Clancy and business icons like the Ford family and Dave Ramsey are the percentage acme of the American engine, they likely represent about 5 percent of a US population now encroaching upon 330 million. Do the math! That's about 16-17 million who gestate and mold the leadership core of the country.

Now compare that to the dual populations of China and India with populations of roughly 1.3 billion each, give or take a million or two. Assume a similar 5 percent "genius quota" in both countries and USA market competitors generate more than 65 million each with the requisite education skill to equal or surpass anything the US propels. The underpinning in both countries, and throughout most Asian communities, is an obsession with formal education that most Americans don't share, particularly in math and science. To resurrect an old cliché, US ineptitude in education is the "canary in the coal mine." In this case it may be the screaming eagle. Other countries require their children and adolescents to spend more time in school and attack a more diverse, difficult curriculum. The US system, however, is very much like a football game where the home team spots the visitors two touchdowns before the opening kick-off, then spends the remaining four quarters scoring from behind.

That needs reversal to assure future success and change our equally clichéd "brain import dependence." Trends in US public education are cyclical, replete with canards like "co-operative learning," "curriculum relevance" and "no child left behind," to name a few. But the real world of economics is much more demanding and unforgiving. Employers could care less about your proficiency with Shakespearean theater, trends in bidets or Gestalt therapy. But what an employer really wants to know is whether you can write a coherent paragraph, analyze a spread-sheet or build an engine part.

"You got'cha no skills; you get'cha no job."

This insight and model I therefore propose began years ago and layers like a vertical bricks wall. Much of the following paradigm is a corollary observation of 28 years as a secondary teacher that I argue Americans ought to adopt.

After a college graduation trip to Europe in the summer of '71, Holland ushered a panoply of insights. The Netherlands, for example, requires all students to study 12 years of English and every Dutch citizen with whom I met spoke it impeccably without trace of accent. Quoting a Dutch businessman, "You Americans only see us through the prism of legal marijuana shops, Amsterdam's 'red light' district and maybe tulips!" His point was that Holland has always been a nation wed to commerce and the sea, and the language of international business, at least at this juncture in the 21th century, WAS English. Much as the anchor of world currency still remains the dollar. I concede that may change by 2050, especially with the assault of the Chinese yuan. But the Dutch government mandated that its citizenry become at least bi-lingual. Most Dutchmen (and women) also speak conversational German and French, a skill partially dictated by the geography of their neighborhood and the history of two world wars.

That experience suggests and cues the model needed to transform the US through the year 2200. So fasten your seat belt, change your azimuth and prepare to gut your perceptions of what public education is…or was. The current model is deficient. The two oceans that once insulated us from the rest of the world are now just large ponds. A recent trip to WalMart will confirm that the invasion is almost complete. Hanes' underwear I just bought, for instance, was made in Vietnam.

How ironic.

What America "invents" is a wealth of ideas. What it "produces" is limited. Note the exit of my hometown of Pittsburgh, PA by the steel industry. The US Steel (now USX) Edgar Thompson works on the Monongehela River is the only one left. Most others have fled to Korea, Birmingham (briefly) and then overseas. It's a sad commentary.

School ought to be an eight-hour day to prepare for a 40-hour work week. Thus the opening bell should start at 8 a.m. and last until 5 p.m. What follows will focus upon the 7th through 12th grade curriculum, the acme of the 12-year pyramid that ostensibly begins at age 5 in Kindergarten. Among the insights bludgeoned upon me in education were those of a German exchange student I taught at West Valley High School in Hemet, CA in the late '90s. He asked to enroll in my freshman "Behavioral Health" class (even as a senior) to polish his English skills because the counselors suggested that might enrich his experience here. He taught me more than I taught him. The stunning part of it was he was, without a doubt, the VERY BEST WRITER OF English of the five classes I then hosted during the school day. Granted even Germany has its share of "dummkopfs" as America, and exchange students, by definition, are almost always superior academic performers. He was, nevertheless, truly exceptional. But he also gave me insight to why he wanted to spend a year in a backwater town like Hemet, California. His insights were remarkable for a kid 17.

German high schools, he said, are more rigorous than American but he also realized that the interlock of European economies was an unavoidable future trend that would shape the lives of every European his age. Senior high school in Germany is FIVE years long and exchange students get NO CREDIT (his citation) toward graduation for their exchange time in the United States. Germany considers our high school system less than appropriately rigorous. Ergo, no credit toward a German diploma!

Germans may be onto something.

He also noted that sports teams at the high school level, unlike the US tradition, affiliate with "clubs" outside of school time. I believe it took West Valley's varsity soccer coach about 10 minutes to discover he was in the student body. Guess who became the varsity goal keeper that year for the West Valley High boys' team that year? It was a no-brainer positive for the program. The three female German exchange students who were also there that year were similar additions to the girls' program and all said they wanted to go undergraduate school here in the United States. Why? They relished the freedom of choice in education that many Americans disdain and perceived school as the advent of opportunity, not some odious albatross to slough off as quickly as possible. The contradiction only underscores the conundrum. German exchange students relish the freedom of the tertiary American universities but their government disdains the American secondary.

He also wanted to travel and his American "host" family accorded him that opportunity. Ten months after arrival, he knew more American history and traveled to more states than 90 percent of his American peers. His stops during school vacations at the Thanksgiving, Christmas and Easter breaks included the Black Hills of South Dakota,

Philadelphia, Washington, D. C. and the Yosemite Valley. I was both humbled and honored to have him in my class.

School should be an 8-hour day beginning at the 7th grade level. Although I can already hear the low moan from the salaried teachers' unions, applause from the hourly support staff and minimal support from the "Imbecile-to-idiot" school administers. Doctorate degrees gave them limited insight into adolescent behavior but buttress their inflated egos about how to teach. Most can tell you seven different ways "how" to teach. But, when you hear one of these paragons spout off about the reform of education, just ask one simple question.

How many years did you actually spend in a classroom in front of real, non-conforming adolescents as a teacher?

It may stun the general public to learn that most "Dud-Fuds" (PhD-types) spent less than four years actually within four walls directing live human beings at the elementary or secondary level. That's part of the problem. Insight and common sense dictate you should have at least 10-12 years of actual classroom experience before any state issues a credential or license to lead. So, before you begin casting aspersions about the failures of subordinate teachers, remember the appropriate Biblical phrase.

"Take the log out of your own eye before you see the splinter in your brother's."

Of all the administrators I met throughout 28 years, only three stood out as stellar. They were Ms. Billie Lutrell at San Gabriel, CA High School in the late 1970s, along with Walt Brubaker and Joe Carlson at the aforementioned Hemet (CA) Unified School District. They were all very different in their approaches and had many critics but effective at what they did. The rest, quoting my son's Baptismal Godfather, Col. John Kaheny, "weren't worth a bucket of warm spit." Kaheny used that phrase in a different context at the conclusion of the Gulf War when we were waiting to rotate back to the states. He then was distressed about the caliber and performance of some of his junior officers in the 3rd Civil Affairs Group both during and after the Gulf War. The unfortunate thing is public education is littered with warm spit, inflated egos and a leadership vacuum that all too often dooms innovation, suppresses dissent and embraces mediocrity.

So how and what to change? And excuse the ellipsis. It's part of my style. Get over it!

Let's start with curriculum about which every dunderhead from principals to sincerely ignorant parents have an "opinion." The new reality is that every student needs to at least be reasonably proficient through at least one year of algebra and a second of geometry. Most state curriculums recognize that and so require. Where the blowout occurs on this freeway is when the student under this mandate fails to achieve that proficiency by this senior year. What do you do then?

What if that student is now a legal adult of 18 or 19? What are his or her viable options?

Currently that student may continue in some adult education context with other "majors" secluded from the bulk of high school students who are "minors." Why? Consider the obvious possibility that a 19 or 20- year-old retained in high school for failure to surpass the math bar has a 14-year-old boyfriend (or girlfriend) with whom they exercise their right of runaway hormones and cavort to cause a teen pregnancy.......or, in the case of a 20-year-old female, a case of statutory rape. This is now the case with those designated as "special education," who may remain in many states at the secondary level until age 22.

How now brown cow?

Although the math requirement is reasonable, it then collides with hormonal reality. Yet the requirement ought to stay because you lie to students if you say proficiency at that level is not necessary. It is and will continue to be. Knowing full well that students will filter into the Adult Education System or college, what essentials must they grasp before their 18th or 19th birthdays in addition to attain requisite math proficiency to function well?

It's pretty obvious that the ability to write a coherent paragraph, summary, e-mail or letter is mandatory, even in the bleak impersonal world of computers and the internet. That's a proficiency rarely obtained in less than four years so the secondary curriculum revolution ought to encompass the following schedule of achieved benchmarks before graduation:

Proficiency at least through elementary geometry and four full years of mathematics. And, no, that inclusive four years does not have to include calculus but some elementary knowledge of statistics.

Language and writing skill sufficient to enter undergraduate program or enter the work world with viable ability to immediately become an asset to real employers who need not have to "un-train" or "retrain" students un-mastered in said.

Physical education mastery of their own bodies with daily physical education that includes nutrition information that equips people for a lifetime of healthy choices. It makes more sense, for example, to promote golf (which I find akin to watching paint dry!), tennis, soccer, basketball, swimming, baseball/softball, track or volleyball, all skills that can be replicated as an adult. And, yes, although I played and still love the game of American football, it makes no sense to spend the exorbitant amount of money necessary to field contact football teams when fewer than one percent of high school graduates will ever play the game again in their lifetime. Relegate it to "club" status where private support provides the necessary structure to allow students to participate. How's that for cultural apostasy!

Real, demonstrated, conversational proficiency in at least one language other than English. Obviously most of America's geography favors Spanish BUT consider at least access to other languages other than Spanish. A cogent example was that of the daughter of a former owner/publisher of the "Grunion Gazette" in Long Beach, CA in the 1980s named John Blowitz whose daughter was a tall blonde senior at Long Beach Milliken High School. She had the foresight to study Japanese for four years in high school and later went to UCLA to expand that proficiency. The world of economics opened up to her at a young age because she was Japanese bilingual and business savvy. Memo to educators in California: There are languages OTS (Other Than Spanish)! Her career in international business, I'm sure, is now meshed in success.

What should also append to the 8-hour school day and rigid academic preparation for undergraduate school is a choice for vocational education that Americans two generations ago chucked aside with the advent of the civil rights movement. The state of California shunned and excised "vocational" education with the fear that it would become the dumping ground for minorities. The thrust then became (and it is) the illusion and ruse that ALL students deserve the panacea of education summoned at Berkeley or UCLA.

Or, as Dr. Phil would say: "How's that workin' for you?"

Thus we now have an entire generation of Americans with "degrees" in psychology, sociology, ecology or some other intense insight into the human soul. Yet they can't fix a faucet, build a sawhorse or change a carburetor simply because we deemed those skills irrelevant to teach in high school. That, I conclude, is gross, group stupidity. The retrograde model to which we ought to revert is to allow at least one site in every public school district to become a campus that teaches the "skills of real life" from electricity to carpentry and plumbing. This was the norm more than two generations ago and I will concur that the politics of union mentoring sometimes interferes rather than promotes the cycle of training new tradesmen (and women). But here's a reality check.

More than 50 years after the remarkable model former California Gov. Pat Brown (not "Moonbeam") set in place with the community college system, we abandoned vocational education at the secondary level. Remember that when you call the "Magtag repair man" to fix your dishwasher. Even better: When you call a plumber because your fecal overload threatens your new carpet. Just be prepared to write that big check because the number of people adequately prepared to service your trade needs is now sorely........

Limited!

Men are Easy:
Food and Sex

That's a **direct quote** from a woman principal at one of the last faculty meetings I attended in Hemet, California. I can't remember whether it was part of her opening monologue or just a throwaway line during the perfunctory after-school discourse. So what's the point?

The faculty audience was exclusively male, testosterone in total, erudite, professional and brimming with "machismo."

We all looked at each other, searching and yearning for the profound insight or snicker. Wake me with an original punch line. "Yeah, so what? I thought that was obvious. Those are my two priorities...... always have been. Depends on how hungry I am. Sex can be the aperitif, the entrée or my particular favorite....the dessert!" Now take that same quote, parse it from the lips of a man to any audience of women or even a co-ed group and what do you have?

Can you say strident, feminist, "Welcome to hell.....in a quick minute, I'm gonna' light a Paula Deen fire under yo'ass " controversy. Marry that to job loss, professional castration, the attendant public flogging and humiliation. If you think we don't have a double-standard here, you did your fair share of undergraduate drugs and your "high" permanently altered your brain housing group. Had a male principal publicly said that in a similar forum, he would be begging to keep his testicles as part of a limited severance package. Part of the workplace problem, in both public and private sectors, is hypersensitivity to correct real harassment with overreaction. Like variants of sexual assault, sexual harassment is vastly underreported. The power vacuum between harasser and the harassed buffers the offender and quells the sunshine on the offense. More legislation and further imposition of "Thou Shalt Not" regulations are flatly lame. Biology almost always trumps imposed rationality and research confirms that we men do have a pre-occupation with sex.

But whatever became of appropriate etiquette, patience and wry humor? Didn't we all have mothers who taught us to disdain bad manners, and not be rude to women? And to one another? I know my Irish-Catholic mother would rail had she confronted similar "breaches of etiquette," a capital sin in her purview that ranked below larceny and just above homicide. We now, however, live in work world where "common sense" is a supremely uncommon and ignored virtue.

Stride the halls of any current junior or senior public high school and prepare to have your ears singed by offensive adolescent conversation. It's all too often vulgar, profane, obscene, sexist and racist. Teachers could spend the bulk of their workday mediating the rude and crude of their class rosters. Such behavior is so prevalent that teachers must commonly ignore it and only confront the most egregious verbal vile. Sending the foul-mouth adolescent to a counselor or vice-principal for insolent, insulting, speech rarely modifies the behavior. They only move it to a different zip code after school.

The incident in graph one only reflects the pervasive epidemic of incessantly bad manners epitomized by insidious entries on "Facebook" and its sister social blogs, sinister networks and websites. Love, hate, vitriol, inspiration and insanity all co-exist in cyberspace where teenagers dwell. So is it a quantum, surprise leap that corruptly bad behavior bleeds onto those who purport to be adults?

Or does that said speech pre-curse the aforementioned overreaction?

Here in the South, I have been addressed as "Hon (pronounced HUN)," "Honey," "Darlin'," "Sweetheart," "Sugar" and "Baby"...... all by myriad women with whom I superficially engaged in a business context. I did not, however, "bitch-slap," hammer, excoriate them or slice and dice their egos over the perceived sexist slight. To again quote a famed rant from the Eagles Glenn Frye and Don Henley: "Get over it"! Whatever it is that trips your dilettante, offensive meter, take a step back, consider the source and don't elevate your diastolic over the trite to trivial. Then take a stand against harassment that is real, pernicious and threatens the well-being of its victims, male or female.

Years ago at UC (Irvine), a woman whom I asked to dinner said she was a feminist and proclaimed "All men are my oppressors." I'd cite her name but this homily protects the names of the ignorant and maladapted. Then she insisted on paying "her" half of the meal, even though I initiated the invite and intended to pay the whole tab. The meal was great at the old "Sid's Blue Beet" in Newport Beach. When she persisted to make an issue of it, I offered to "really" liberate her and let her pay the entire bill. Hesitation ensued. Don't remember where the conversation went thereafter.

But I hope she coughed up the cash and left a good tip with her declaration of feminism.

At some point in human history we all need to exhale, get off whatever pedestals we cherish and relish good manners, good humor and laughter. I suspect most folks with an agenda on their chests don't realize how obnoxious they've become with their feigned role of victim when the rest of us have to tolerate their own scorecard of insults (see Occupy Wall Street for confirmation). Most of us tire of the self-perceived, odious mantle of martyrdom these social misfits impose on society. To the several women I've encountered who deploy this tactic: Stuff it in your moon chute, then retrofire! To the many males I've met intoxicated by their own vanity: Quit with the self-proctology! Your head is so far north, you could be doing your own liver biopsy. Identify the examples of insulting insensitivity prevalent throughout the culture. Then avoid them.

Years ago at one of those onerous "wine and cheese" gatherings at the University of Arizona, the guest of honor was an architect named Ray Romero whom I interviewed for one of the publications of UA's Department of Journalism. His phenomenal work, a scale model of a forthcoming project, was part of the artistic display. During the exchange, a young woman joined the conversation, then steered it in a different direction. Ignorance then percolated to the surface.

"How long have YOUR PEOPLE (emphasis mine) been in this country?" Yes, she actually posed the question! Although I found her approach jolting, insulting and inane, Ray handled it with class. He was a 7th-generation Mexican-American, who spoke limited Spanish, a graduate of UA who owned his own thriving architecture firm. The reaction was disarming. He just smiled and intoned.

"Since 1804!"

Oops! The woman squirmed nervously on her four-inch heels, immediately realized her faux pas, muttered something randomly incoherent and quietly faded into the brie crowd for another glass of wine. Hope that cheese modified her lack of tact. I doubt she recognized how embarrassed we were for her. She was ignorance cloaked in a tight dress with a plunging neckline and a great derriere (Size 4 as I recall). Ray made no issue of the unsubtle incident and chalked it off to the complementary wine. And allow a quote from the script of one of Paul Newman's best films, "Hud."

"What we have 'y 'here', is failure to communicate!"

My own wife, Anita Louise Rodriguez, whose mother's maiden name was Villasenor, remembers similar, abrasive insults and reminded me the other day of a similar drive-by slur. One of my long term friends from my Disneyland days long ago once asked her when he first met her: "Where were you born?" The inference was what? North or South of the Mexican border? To clear the record once and for all time: Anita's parents, Elvira Villasenor and Joe Rodriguez, were also born in the US, he in Los Angeles and she in the then territory of New Mexico. One of Anita' uncles (Ray Villasenor) survived the Bataan Death March, then became a career Army enlisted until retirement in the mid-60s. Another of Vera's cousins was in the Army Air Corps and shot down over the South Pacific. And all five of the Rodriguez family children are college graduates: Two from the University of Southern California and three from Long Beach State University.

And.......by the way......men ARE easy. Just let a little humor prevail over your sensitive egos. And always remember that a good meal should introduce an even better dessert. And that doesn't mean "Baked Alaska"!

Winter Katrina 2009

For those bi-coastal Narcisstic, Ivy League Brahmins who missed the "Great Kentucky Ice Storm" of 2009, suppress a laugh, meander through Al Gore's greatest invention (The Internet) and peruse the pictures. While the country was righteously aghast at the nightmare of Hurricane Katrina in 2008, behold the parallel destruction of mid-America in January of the ensuing year.

It got virtually no attention from the drive-by, mainstream media and even less from the packrats at the Federal Emergency Management Agency.

Sean Padraic Fitch (that's John Patrick in Gaelic!) correctly scored the storm as "Obama's Winter Katrina." He happens to be my son. George Bush Jr. and the elected Louisiana cretins, who ran the real estate Jefferson pilfered from Napoleon to pay France's then war debt, were collectively absent in 2008. More than a century later, American politicians of all persuasions drank the shrill swill of Katrina's dance through the Bayou. Those in charge blew it. Their ineptitude deserves no defense. Those at state and city levels acted like petulant adolescents, attempting to shift all blame for their pathetic response onto the Federal Government.

The governor, the mayor of "N'awOrlins" (pronounce it right, ya'll!), Louisiana's two U. S. Senators and every Federal bureaucrat in

Federal Emergency Management (a.k.a. Moron) Agency seemed to visit all too many of the ubiquitous "Drive-Through-Daiquiri" shops that dot "N'awOrlins." FEMA's tepid arrival was galling at best and bungled at worst. Local government failed at almost all critical points. Except the U. S. Coast Guard and other military personnel, the death toll in Louisiana would have exceeded levels even more appalling than the 1,400 plus who needlessly died.

Although party animals consider the city a strangely enlightened ode to "Les Bon Temps," it amazes me that the folks of New Orleans suffered through the flood waters, the sewage, the breakdown of civility, the 'gators and runaway cottonmouths to manage a comeback. Kudos to Harry Connick Jr., the Neville family et al. who returned for the resurrection and the New Orleans Saints for leading the salvation of the city's drowning soul. The healing after Katrina became one of those great paeans to the diversity of American culture un-replicated anywhere else in North America. The Marine Corps exposed me to some of this cultural dynamic while I spent time there on active duty in the '90s.

The music, the art and the lovable vulgarity of Bourbon Street are sheer delights that defy logic. The strange habit of women on balconies "flashing" above the most famed rue in the whole South is crass, brazen entertainment, a sheer evocation of the bawdy. "Ain't nuthin' like Bourbon St.!" anywhere else in the United States. Just walk its few short blocks almost any night of the week and marvel at its lovable scatology. I experienced said on active duty in 1993.

"Show us your tits (really spelled teats), show us your tits," the crowds yelled......and, almost on cue, voluptuous young women would entertain the crowd below with some very adorable mammaries and memories! Savoring their victory of persuasion, the crowd always grew bolder along with the subsequent chants:

"Show us your bush, show us your bush!" And we ain't talkin' presidents 41 and 43 here!

Thus, for all you Methodist mothers from Iowa and the rest of middle-America who think their daughters are terminal virgins, I must tell you....we saw lots of "bush," both combed and shaven. The theater here is that there are cops (real and fake) who feign to restrain or arrest these miscreants, pretend to be offended and then politely ignore the intrusion of nudity.

What are the "rewards" for all this flashing?

Beads! Thousands and thousands of decorative beads ascend to the balconies so the triumphant ladies can collect their "loot." I must admit I saw many Iowa blue-hair grandmas who pretended to be shocked by the politely lewd, semi-lascivious, innocuous behavior. Now what the hell the women do with all those beads remains a mystery to explore with the natives? You can't turn them over for cash at the U. S. Mint.

I couldn't resist.

Turning to one of the offended, post-menopausal mamas, her mouth agape at the ghastly display, I directed her to the other end of Bourbon Street were there are a collection of "Gay bars" where she could witness a similar, bizarre display of male anatomy. Hey, Bourbon Street is an equal-opportunity offender! The good times roll both ways. No discrimination here. Her face turned pale, she snorted something under her breath while grabbing her aging, balding husband to leave. What he really needed was a subscription to the "Hair Club for Men" and a shot of fellatio.

But he would hear none of it. Like most of his male counterparts on the street, he was in the "throes of party." His gaze was on the balcony above.

Our "Ice Storm" had none of those delightful melodramatics as frigid weather, no heat and cooking in a burn barrel with some of our many downed oak trees was a camping trip I choose to forego and forget. But I couldn't. Despite what they proclaim, Marines, young and old, can tolerate almost anything if they see a positive conclusion on the horizon. Yet, after seven days of sleeping in a sweat suit, encased in sleeping bag, with my favorite size-6, 55-year-old Latina "hottie," it gets very old and still very cold. Never accorded cold weather training with the Corps at Bridgeport, CA, I can honestly say: "I'll pass!" Self-imposed discomfort is not my strong suit.

The Kentucky National Guard arrived on schedule (five days late) after the storm hit. Unlike residents of N"awlins, locals in McCracken County broke out their chainsaws, cleared the roads and driveways of debris and reached out to their neighbors. The horrifying images of police who abandoned their posts, the anarchy and "'gators in the water" were not part of the Kentucky experience. But the threat posed by the freezing temperatures was unique and, although not as deadly, had similar potential. At midnight of the storm's first day, I stood in our driveway and listened to power transformers perched on utility lines explode like artillery shells. It sounded very much like the experience I witnessed during the Tet Offensive of 1968. You can even call it a "flashback." There are fewer things that will tighten all bodily apertures more than like the decibel whistle of "incoming." Sphincter control may not be an option. Couple those signature sounds with that of falling limbs weighted with chains of ice and suddenly you had a cacophony that mimicked a real battle zone. The contrast in response to the disaster here is an abject lesson in preparation and subsequent reaction. The emergency response here at the state and county level was 180 degrees removed from the static, inert and sometimes lame behavior of their N"awlins counterparts.

We saw no swarms of national media during the storm and the ensuing destruction of the electrical grid. Remember, this is the Kentucky only recognized as a flyover state that the Media Morons of New Amsterdam only considered a throwaway collection of modern troglodytes. Most of that bicoastal crowd still thinks Kentucky has only three memorable citizens: Daniel Boone, Daniel Webster and Henry Clay. Aside from a classic basketball program at the state university and the Kentucky Derby, what else does the state have to offer besides Mint Juleps? But pay attention, ya'll! What the storm became was a harbinger of what could be in a widespread war or future attacks by Islamo-Fascist fanatics.

Imagine your world without electricity.

No lights, no heat, no gas pumps, no ATMs, no cash registers and no Wal-Marts.

Now imagine it for three weeks. Yes, the storm did that!

Then imagine that condition as a permanent fixture of the landscape. No electrical grid indefinitely. Good luck to America's many urban areas and welcome to strident chaos!

Homey Don't Face, Homey Don't Tweet and Homey Don't Text

(With due apologies to Keenan Ivory Wayans!)

Consider life before Microsoft, Google, Facebook and the perversions of alleged "social media." Then permit a homily about the annoying rash of technology that strangles the 21st century. Although we antique Luddites embrace the sacred nuance of the digital, do not presume our protocol subscription is eternal. The vogue addiction to the toys of cyberspace creates a real barrier to inter locution, an invisible barricade that segregates us all. Why talk or converse when you can "actually" send a text message and be completely impersonal?

Then meld "carpel thumb syndrome" (the dreaded CTS) to the addiction of the internet and we humans become indentured servants to "APPS" that do everything from create our friends to our menu choices. For all the marvels of Facebook, its unique design and applications, Zuckerburg & Co. likely never realized or cared about the implication that "friends together" also built new walls of separation and a permanent corruption of privacy. If they did, their direction was pernicious even as they considered it benign. It was just another venal victim of the law of unforeseen consequences. Even "privacy" as legal jargon did not enter the Supreme Court's lexicon until the 1890s. Now we have the famous quote more than a decade ago by the then "El Jefe" of Yahoo, here paraphrased.

"The era of privacy is over. Get used to it."

He interjected that flip comment in a mid-90s press conference with an attitude rife with callous indifference. For that enunciation of the obvious, he endured resounding criticism. The current generation of android addicts now reaps the chafe of whatever they sowed on Facebook. Its content eventually morphs into public fodder with anything from humor to rancor. And, yes, the site does allow for "private conversations." But what about storage of the text and who, besides its creator, knows who else reads it? As now revealed, everyone from the NSA to the CIA, IRS and myriad members of the alphabet soup, others are all privy to your privacy. Is it communication or a library of insults/defamations open to all? Anything a subscriber puts on Facebook subjects him or her to the laws of libel and the scrutiny of myriad government snoops. Granted it will be difficult to bring judgment upon a defendant who lives halfway around the world, but not impossible. Plaintiffs with big money and larger egos will find a way. It's the new National Enquirer! Like slander, words that pass the lips are impossible to retract, retrieve and amend. And now that the "Feds," potential employers, police departments and competent criminals all have access to this open information, welcome to a new warning label: Caveat scriptor! (Let the writer beware!). Also remember that what you put on Facebook becomes THEIR property. Hope you read the fine print. Mark the Z owns the stuff you voluntarily surrendered to him.

Aside from the loss of privacy, the "Millenials" that spawned Occupy Anything from Wall St. to the Outhouse will discover, to their grief, is real rejection. Like Irish nudists at New York's St. Patrick's Day parade on a 32-degree day, their limitations become public view. Their inclusion in the macro-economy might suffer the stain of the Narcisstic camp crusade circa 2011-2012. Potential employers do "mine" the internet and remain suspect of hiring someone who adorns the mantle of anti-capitalism. The lesson Millenials forgot with a brain cramp in econ class was that everyone first acts in their own self- interest, hopefully within the parameters of ethical behavior. Running amuck on Facebook and taking cheap shots at people, reeks of the brusquely juvenile. Those who employ will treat those who defame like a bad skin rash that may need scratched but they'll offer no salve.

Privacy and mining, however, don't begin to address the digitized stupidity of "YouTube" public nudity, indecency and sexual trysts online. In an era of cell phones with cameras: "Don't do anything in public that you wouldn't do in front of your mother in your grandmother's kitchen."

That's "Patrick's Classroom Rule."

Then, years later, you can avoid some of those intrusive, embarrassing questions posed by your adolescent sons and daughters along with their pubescent friends.

"Hey mom, is that really you in this picture?

"I didn't know you shaved down there. And who's that nude guy you're with? That ain't dad!"

"I didn't know you smoked!"

Funny how some uncomfortable conversations start.

Then add to the Facebook pandemic the phenomenon of Twitter, a vehicle poised to destroy the notion of orthographic spelling (i.e. correctly-spelled words!). Quoting the company's opening pitch, it says "at the heart of Twitter are small bursts of information called Tweets." "Small" is too expansive to describe a Tweet as the information bytes mandated by Twitter that must have no more than 140 "characters," or word(s) often with mere phonetic spellings, abbreviations or "grunts" like OMG (Oh, my God!) and LMAO (Laughed my ass off!). It is language spiraled downward to its lowest common denominator under the guise of communication. Yet here it hyperventilates through the ruins of cyberspace, taking no prisoners with euthanasia of all language precise.

Now this kind of contorted sentence structure was maybe not what the purveyors of Twitter intended. Their enlightened attempt was to create a platform, vehicle or structure, with which people could exchange information, both verbal and visual, in a compact way without clutter. The Twitter "Tweets" paradigm was much like the Hallmark concept with greeting card commentary. Say what you need to transmit as succinctly as possible. That, however, also caters to the gargle, groans and retching of pedestrian conversation devoid of sentence enveloped in fragments. Listen to most adult conversation. Normally it is composition of phrases, grunts and exclamations, not soliloquy. Now it's traded on the New York Stock exchange. Last quote I heard was $38 per share in 2015. P.T. Barnum was right. And its addicted audience abounds. Welcome to 2016!

The brilliance of the Tweet concept, however, is an outgrowth of the original "Life Magazine" of the '50s where pictures were the focus with the adjunct verbal commentary relegated to minimal. It is the visual without the clutter of the words needed to convey ideas and meaning. Even for the most verbose among us, Twitter has an almost hormonal attraction at the ease with which you can flash your commentaries, inane or otherwise, throughout the globe to an audience of one...or millions. Just ask Donald Trump! It just doesn't ring my inspiration bell. It's more akin to profanity and obscenity where a short phrase is acceptable and telegraphs what you really mean without much premeditation. You just blurt it out! Blurts are now the Tweets of cyberspace and a new word added to the ever-expanding lexicon of acceptable English.

As a professor friend at New Mexico Tech so eloquently put into anecdote, now visualize the phenomenon of "texting." The word image he painted was that of his two sons at the graduation party he and his wife hosted for the youngest years ago. Their large home had the requisite share of future college freshmen and peers of his older, matriculating brother from New Mexico State. Frank first noticed an awkward silence during the middle of the party. Why? It seems the bulk of those in attendance were in different parts of the same house furiously thumbing their way into cyberspace to connect with peers 10 to 50 feet away. Like an order of Trappist monks, the silence broached deafening, unlike the normal "raconteur" you would expect from a cabal of collegians. The cell phone madness gripped the attendees and thumbs shuttered at Mach 1 speed to convey information into an adjacent room. Dad watched the exercise with humor and reminded me why he forbids all such devices during the conduct of his college classes. They are a distraction in that forum and equally so at social gatherings. Now we have the bad habit of a new generation that disdains conversation and opts to hurl a text in lieu of the opening "Hello" to the last "Goodbye". On the brighter side of this cyber-thrust, it probably makes divorce and custody arguments much more original. Why talk to your ex-whatever when you can just blow him or her off with a "text'?

Like it or not, it is part of the new stupidity that separates us as human beings. Why bother with conversation when you can text? It is, however, an efficient option to convey information outside of normal business hours as the cell phone is a 24/7 blunt instrument. That access has some merit as calling your boss with a great idea at 2 a.m. generates no warmth or love. But it will be there with his or her morning coffee and today's Wall Street Journal by 7 a.m. when reception is a propos. Thus a "text" is a mixed blessing. As a designated hitter for conversation, it's batting below the Mendoza line but occasionally whacks one out of the park.

Just don't make it a habit that sheds like a snake with old skin.

Life by One-Third(s)

Although all stereotypes are 10 percent true, the flawed perspective from Baby-Boomers to Millenials reinforces the bias. There are three groups of people who inhabit this hallowed planet: "Those who make it happen; those who watch it happen; and those who ask: Wa'happened?"

The sad state of contemporary, maybe declining, America is that the entitlement society of the latter group threatens to immerse ambition, productivity and common sense. As of this date of this writing in February, 2012, the Washington Times carried a dripping commentary sympathetic to the plight of a 2008 graduate of Yale University awarded a master's in fine arts now working for $9/hr. at a photo lab. The writer's opinion hemorrhaged the story with retching sympathy. She expanded the graduate's individual plight to include the exponential plight that afflicts an entire generation of Millenials groping for promised careers fed by a lifetime diet of expectation now morphed into anger that spawned the Occupy Wall Street idiocy. It may be a lesson learned late in life but learn it now before age 35 as the discomfort of the present should lead to creative exits forward. Hunger is a powerful incentive. The real world of economics holds your liberal arts degrees with distain and less reverence than a Pyongyang driver's license. The degree is the starting block, not the victory tape. The "rights and privileges thereunto pertaining" will take a lifetime to evolve. Success means deflating your ego with a modicum of humility. The vaunted baccalaureate only announces your entry to the race. It does not assure the laurels of victory. The sooner Millenials make the confession, the less onerous the penance. Then it is easier to devise a rational solution or plan for career. Yes, the country is/was in the midst of a great recession. How profound that "fall back" augurs for the future is the playground for historians. And for those of us who remember the horrid recession of the Jimmy Carter era circa 1979 to 1982, 2012 is equally traumatic. Can anyone remember 20 percent interest rates on mortgages? I do. But who will succeed and shake the discomfort of their current state, make no excuse and shuttle forward?

Will it be those of the one-third who really make it happen? Or will it be the troubled ones who ask "What happened?" as 2020 speeds past them?

Waiting for economic opportunity like some trolley scheduled to transport you to Nirvana is car fare to insanity. Millenials, including my kids, with the wherewithal to garner a degree also possess a compendium of skills for transit to a different space. That then ignites the strategy to change the focus, alter a previous mindset and set new goals and directions. Thus your taste for latte in New York City might require a career shift and years in the winter purgatory of Bismarck, North Dakota. Fed by the hallucinogens of their parents my age, we of "Baby-Boomer persuasion," Millenials really expected a smooth transition to a life of entitled prosperity and unparalleled opportunity. Just check with Bernie Sanders and "Feel the Bern." That doesn't mean it can't happen but maybe a new roadmap is in order. MapsQuest ceded to Google Maps and we all survived. That Nirvana trolley may not run with the precision of the national German rail system. It may be more like that of Greece and Pakistan, addicted to the inefficient and tardy. But get on the train you must and proceed to make a difference. That's what the one-third do. They take the hand dealt and move forward.

Then consider those whose lot in life is to "watch" it happen. They will likely obtain a modicum of success...... but at what price? Waiting for those to provide "for you" with a career or job is the crass equivalent of confinement to a plantation as an indentured servant. The lament of "I need a job!" allows opportunity to flee personal responsibility. You wait while some one else defines your life, your choices, your career because you cede those decisions to others by proxy. Much of this mindset permeates the union movement where members expect others to open the door to them for assigned work or direction. If you are a truly competent and astute carpenter, for example, why should you need to go to the "union hall" to seek work? Unless your seniority status puts you at the head of the line of selection, your subsets of skills matter little when those of less competence acquire the assigned work. If you can't effectively use a framing square, you shouldn't even be in the business of building. Although now retired, I was a lifelong AFL-CIO member. We members all witnessed the irony of the less competent selected over the more is a conundrum never addressed by the labor movement. First in line, first hired. Last in line, first fired. It's the epitaph of a dying movement. Seniority alone rewards only the ossified mind and the inert, inept performance.

The "watch" category now counts those of my post-war generation from the United Steel Workers (USW) to the United Mine Workers suffering from the intentional persecution of the Obama administration. Coal is still exiting in limited volume but moving down the Ohio through the Mississippi bound for places like South Africa where the need for coal-fired heat is still a priority. The United Mines Workers are now the pallbearers at their own funeral, spectators to the migration of their jobs to places in Asia, the Caribbean and Africa with names that they cannot even pronounce. Just today on my re-edit of this segment, (7 Feb. 2016) Ford announced they will build a brand new factory in old Mexico to produce 500,000 new units for sale.

I just can't wait to hear the caterwauling from the UAW.

The golden goose of steel died in my hometown of Pittsburgh more than two generations ago and thousands "watched" it happen, dazed, confused and angry. The only thing "steel" about Pittsburgh is now the football team. The neighborhood around the U. S. Steel (now USX) Edgar Thompson Works on the edge of town is a dilapidated slum that once housed a vibrant middle class and now stands as testimony to decline. It's more Detroit than center Pittsburgh whose vibrant recovery still remains threatened by a dwindling tax base.

In 1891, there were 56 mills in the greater Pittsburgh area. During the '50s and '60s, the summertime night skies bled beautiful hues of red, orange and yellow at night from the smokestacks on the Monongahela that fed the businesses and taverns on the South Side of the river. And, yes, that steel production indeed gestated lung and water pollution. Yet there was a demand during the summer for college students then to work at $14-$17/hr. to replace steelworkers on vacation, enjoying the deserved fruits of an industry booming as late as the early '60s.

No mas! Yeah, bass fishing is back in the Monongahela River that now is the favored menu item for the returning bald eagles nesting in the cliffs above. It's a tribute to both the Pennsylvania Game Commission and the EPA. Up until this year, it had been more than 150 years since America's bird lived on that river bank. Conservation works.

Score one for both bird and fish. But the industrial jobs.......they're ancient history.

Then there is frightening encroachment of the one-third who bypassed progress, ambition and hustle. The stark reality of the "unemployment" numbers that began their escalation after the Wall Street meltdown of 2008 are figures camouflaged to fit whatever agenda whatever politicians cite. The Department of Labor publishes a quarterly cocoon of lies designed to deflate the joy of the jobless. After six months, those who surrendered to the despair fostered by "unemployment checks" wallow in the downward spiral no longer even counted as unemployed. They are left to the government heroin of 99 weeks. Surrender to the Federal needle of addiction and the need for work becomes numb.

That dog, however, won't hunt (to morph another cliché) for anyone who fell into the abyss of the unemployed. Like deer in the headlights, they stand frozen and static, waiting for the lifeguard of government to rescue them from themselves. They feel cheated and project their lack of success upon the sins and avarice of others, aka the One Percent. Maybe the Donald is the Messiah! Locked in their own mindset of desperation, the corrupted vision they've adopted needs to exit the miasma of failure that consumes them like a tsunami. It's as much a dirth of dollars as death of the soul. Outside, macro-solutions don't exist. Imposition of the drive to succeed is fantasy. If you wish to exit the pain of the present toward a richer future, the engine of change is in your hands and head. Life is not static and change only when it happens in the mind and heart.

I'm just not sure we're there yet.

Myriad Flavors of Christianity

If you thought "39 Flavors Ice Cream" had the monopoly on multiple choice, visit the religion section of the McCracken County (KY) phonebook. There are enough variants of "Christians" throughout the South to give Jesus, much less his Father, a migraine headache. They range from your standard hues of Protestant, Presbyterian, Baptist, Methodists and Catholic through a maze of the New Testament obscure like the "New Geneva Community Church" in Paducah and a church designed and catering to Harley-Davidson bikers with a real Harley that anchors the pulpit.

Welcome to Sundays with the confusing array of visitors to Noah's Ark of Christian belief!

In a commonwealth like Kentucky (that comprise four of the 50 states), where the median family income of four is slightly more than $37,000 per annum in 2016, the majority Christian of all variants render allegiance to Jesus, Gin Mills and liquor outlets. Elmer Gantry and his Redneck cousins show up on the county line three miles from our house next to the neighboring four liquor stores and tavern/bar/saloon(s) for the mandatory Tent City Revival near the end of every summer solstice. Their mission on the McCracken-Graves County divide is to "save your soul," expand their following and fill the collection basket. What's a good sermon without the perfunctory passing of the plate once or twice? You can then take the 5-minute pedestrian walk to the "Smoke Shop" or 1241 Liquor to quench your thirst for tobacco and alcohol. Not recommended, however, is crossing Highway 45 to the east where two of the four dens of iniquity house their deadly store of bibacious swill and tobacco. Unless confined within a steel cage on four wheels, traverse not "45" on foot. No light; no crosswalk; no chance. Become a casualty at your own risk.

So I find the juxtaposition hysterically funny: Three alcohol/tobacco outlets less than 500 yards apart in a county with only 55,000 people ? Get some Jesus; get some beer. Then chomp on whatever tobacco variant lights your fire. The bifurcation reeks of "non compos mentis." It's more like an incursion into Dante's 7th Tier of Hell. Hope many of the methamphetamine freaks, who call McCracken home, showered and made it to the tent revival before "chuggin'" some of the state's finest bourbon. Google it! There are, at this juncture, at least 12 bourbon distilleries in this commonwealth. Now I know South-Central Los Angeles has more liquor outlets than the entire state store system total in Pennsylvania, but three within walking distance? If nothing else, overkill is a sacrament Kentucky reveres on multiple levels. Try this on for size. There are 120 counties in Kentucky.Seventy of them are "dry."

Say what, 'homeboy'!

"It's the "state" of Kentucky when they tax or impose fees," a friend from Graves County said, "but it's the 'commonwealth' when they owe the poor taxpayer." You'll feel the full weight and force of their ability to extract when you owe but the commonwealth suffers amnesia when they owe you. This taxpayer, however, has a different bent. Kentucky refunds arrive much more rapidly than the parent IRS. Since the USPS plans no more overnight delivery, that "check in the mail" downshifts to low gear with your vaunted income-tax refund. Smart Kentuckians receive it via internet bank transmission. They make the IRS look like the last girl asked to dance, poorly dressed and ugly. Kentucky always delivers before the Federal return.

Then couple your Bible with the cult of pastor personality and you have the full church spectrum , each of which portends to be the one true roadmap to celestial bliss post mortality. There is a plethora of pastors throughout the South (and elsewhere) who suffer from HVF (high vanity factor). That might impede their seat selection at the Eternal World Series. Those who think they have box or reserve seats may suddenly discover on the Final Judgment Day that they barely made it to the top row of the bleachers with their incursion into the bullpen of avarice and pride. Humility is often not their strong suit. That choice of capital sins, however, doesn't impede the length or sophorous content of their message. The chorus of "My God's Bigger than Your God, My God's Bigger than yours" falls on a cathedral of deaf ears immune to the ecumenical spirit of where Christianity ought to be. The cochophany of "true believers" on Sunday does not include those of Hebrew persuasion, much less adherents of Islam. Note also the infliction of AM radio and Jesus cable TV with the entire choir of cable preachers. I may not get CNN if I don't pay my satellite bill but I still get Jimmy Swiggart's son and his Sunday AM competition with the harangue to repent . It gives "choice" a new meaning. To corrupt a '60s cliché: "Turn on, tune in and tune out!" Open a storefront, grab a Bible and get a CPA! Now you're in business. Despite the multitude of rocks tossed at competing religions, adherents convinced of the efficacy of their Biblical brand ought to live the phrase.

"Let he who is without sin cast the first stone!"

And that doesn't just include adultery.

Thank you, Messrs. Clinton, Kennedy and Johnson!

Maybe the deadliest sin, particularly in small communities throughout both the South and the rest of America, is "Thou Shalt Not Bear False Witness." Christians who flog other Christians for whatever reason need to re-check their celestial destination ticket. Destruction of a reputation pre-curses destruction of the soul. Awkward, isn't it: Christians wailing on other Christians because they wear a different cloth hewn from the rock of St. Peter? The media excoriates the faith of then Denver quarterback Tim Tebow, yet politely ignores the intrusions by Muslims in New York City who impose their faith by blocking pedestrians and traffic while at prayer at their mosques. Christians need to embrace the totality of its faith from foundation to 2016. That includes "all Christians," not just those you deem "sufficiently Christian." ISIS has already published your death warrants, you rancid infidels. Thirty-nine congregations at the foot of the same cross ought to recognize one another, not turn the other cheek in distain. Don't Catholics, Presbyterians, Methodists, Anglicans and Baptists have more in common than not? Sounds like the 2012 Florida Republican primary! Talk to one another. Conversation is productive.

Then there's the dwindling attendance factor.

Add to that collection of God's children those who only appear at baptisms, weddings and funerals. It's the syndrome decried by pastors of all stripes who only "hatch, match and dispatch" as a lifelong friend, fellow seminarian and priest who married us so elegantly phrased it. They see their pew mongers only at baptisms, weddings and the eventual funeral. Then exhume the disturbing face of Christians confined to their self-imposed, chosen catacombs.

Churches may also be the last remnant of segregation here in the South. Just check the color spectrum on Sunday mornings. You will find the "self-segregation" of the congregations therein depressing. There are four AME (Anglican-Methodist-Episcopal) churches here whose congregants are almost exclusively black. They are seldom seen at the rest of Baptist-Catholic-Episcopal-Methodist-Lutheran Sundays on the eccglesial pulpits that sadly remains all-white. That might make a 30-something Nazarene weep in despair. It wasn't what He intended.

I thought Heaven was color blind.

If all Christians emanate from the message of Jesus Christ, why has the vanity of the Valkyries separated us all?

Marine to Anteater to Rag Picker

After the return to CONUS (Continental United States in '68), I called my mother in Pittsburgh to assure her that we arrived safely from Okinawa. She asked me where my next duty station would be. All Naval personnel get to submit a "dream sheet" through the chain of command about where they wanted to deploy before transfer orders arrive. I had pulled off an admission to the University of Califonia (Irvine) by neglecting to mention that I had been "suspended" (actually thrown out) of Catholic University in Washington, D. C. for which I had a bad lapse of memory. I could never remember what I did those 1.5 years there and just forwarded my transcript from Villanova where I spent my freshman year from '62-'63 with a 3.1 Grade Point Average. I told them I'd spent four years in the Corps and only one year in college. The nightmare of Catholic U. with a 1.6 GPA is not worth rekindling. Three weeks to the day of my application to UC, the acceptance letter arrived at Khe Sanh in early December of '67, just before the Siege.

I requested El Toro first, Camp Pendleton or Twentynine Palms on my "dream sheet" to be near UC (Irvine). The old Marine Corps Air Station at El Toro was fewer than 10 minutes from the now sprawling campus with of more than18,000 students. Then it was the newest campus of the statewide system at that time with a mere 1,800. I was part of the class of '71.

So, in typically Corps fashion, the orders were to report to Marine Corps Air Station, Cherry Point, NC. They did that as matter of course to pay the shortest travel mileage to your home of contract record at the end of enlistment. North Carolina to Pittsburgh was a lost less final, travel pay "jing" to move someone back home than California to the 'Burgh.

To my delight and surprise my mother then read a letter from then California U. S. Senator Thomas Kuechel that confirmed that the Corps changed my duty station orders from Cherry Point to El Toro after she asked him to intervene in a very articulate letter that outlined why. She argued that my acceptance into UCI, survival of the horror of the Tet Offensive and Siege at Khe Sanh that I at least deserved that nominal courtesy on my last six months of active duty near the campus. Kuechel concurred and so intervened with Headquarters, Marine Corps. There was only one "hitch in the get-along." I had to report to the nearest Marine Corps Reserve Center in the Oakland district of Pittsburgh near the University of Pittsburgh and get an "administra-tive/modification" of the orders before returning to California. Two days later, the Inspector-Instructor staff First Sergeant of what I re-member as a reserve motor pool unit berated me for 10 minutes as a "shitbird Marine" who had to hide behind his mother's skirt and a Con-gressional intervention. If this paragon of a staff non-commissioned of-ficer is still alive today and reads this, I have two words for him.

And it ain't "Welcome to New York!"

He was another pathetic example of the multitude of poor en-listed leaders that the Corps needed to flush into the septic system from the ranks during the '70s. I endured his ignorance and moved on to the next phase of life at El Toro Marine Corps Air Station and UCI.

By that time I was savvy to the subtle nuances of military "admin" when I reported to the Headquarters Squadron, Headquarters Group, 3rd Marine Aircraft Wing as the group's legal court reporter in late April of '68. I only reported to the wing administration and the wing "disbursing" unit to assure I got paid. The day after my arrival, I was ordered to the commanding officer's office along with the group Sergeant Major. The CO asked me in some detail about my experience with 1/26 at Khe Sanh, seemed genuinely impressed, turned to the sergeant major and said "Promote this Marine to sergeant."

His terse response: "But he doesn't have the 'cutting score,' sir, and not enough time-in-grade." Remember, this was the same SNCO who met us on the tarmac during deplaning. He did not remember me. Then, right before my eyes, the lieutenant colonel opened my Service Record Book (SRB) and proceeded to change the previous proficiency and conduct evaluation scores that ranged from one to four (four being best) with white-out and a black pen. I now had the appropriate cutting score! When he finished, he handed the SRB to the sergeant major. "Prepare the warrant, sergeant major, and call a group formation tomorrow for the promotion ceremony." That was an officer with vision. Ceremony over the next day, I reported to the group legal office with a staff of two: Myself and a major who was on the commanding general's shit list.

The major was a jet jockey and "short-timer" about to leave active duty and go to grad school at the University of Southern California. Like me, he also had the requisite short-timer disposition accentuated when ordered to report into a CH-46 helicopter unit in Tustin, CA upon his return from Vietnam. Appearing before the 3rd MAW commanding general, he sealed the remainder of his fate on active duty when he told the CG:

"This Marine doesn't fly rotary rocks, sir!"

It's never an enlightened idea to piss off a general-grade officer, so the CG made the major suffer through the requisite "attitude correction speech," banished him to be the Headquarters Group legal officer for the remainder of his tour and took him OFF flight status, essentially a forced reduction in pay. So there we were in legal purgatory, assigned to adjudicating the administration of minor infractions and special courts-martial. But anytime a charge sheet came to my desk, I strongly "suggested" to the major that he recommend to any of the squadron COs in the group that a hearing for Office Hours or Captain's Mast, as the squids call it, in lieu of a court. Have them handle it. Neither one of us wanted to shuffle the paperwork associated with a court-martial…
…particularly if that meant deferring the dates forward for our EASs (End of Active Service) in September that would have extended our exit dates until conclusion of any trial.

So we had this tentative working arrangement where I would take off for the beach to do "functional" things like look for housing after active duty and I believe the major used to have a Thursday T-time every week. Effectively we worked four days a week but still managed to cover the requirements of the office. It was more telling about the real time pace of the work than it was about our slovenly commitment. I also admit to a perfectly legal scam where I would schedule Office Hours or proposed Special Courts-Martial on days where I was to be the Sergeant-of-the Guard for the headquarters group, essentially a glorified phone watch that would last 24-hours. I would then go to the same sergeant major referenced heretofore on the tarmac after the flight home and announce the day before that I couldn't stand the duty as I was the group's only legal administrator. That worked....for about four months.

Then, one day in later July, the aforementioned, cigar- chomping fat man discovered the scam and stormed into our little office, bellowing and braying.

"Sergeant Fitch, you haven't checked out a rifle!"

Pause for effect. I couldn't resist.

"You mean we do that kind of thing here in the air wing, sergeant major?"

There ensued, thereupon, a professional "ass-chewing" that inside made me smile. He prattled on for a good three-five minutes (about average for an ass-chewing) and I enjoyed it ever so much. The net result was that, for the last six weeks I spent on active duty, my favorite sergeant major came to our office at 1500 every Wednesday and marched me over to the wing armory where he watched me re-clean an M-14 rifle that likely had not seen a 7.62 round pass through its barrel within the previous decade. It was form of professional harassment but I made sure that the weapon was one antiseptic, operating room clean. Still the sergeant major had further Marine "motivation" on tap for what he perceived as a poor attitude on the part of the rookie, misfit E-5.

Marines then, under normal conditions, had to go to the rifle range annually to re-qualify. Since I had fewer than eight weeks left on active duty, he couldn't lay that gig on me. It would be a waste of ammunition. After all, I did drill two NVA and sent them forth to the afterlife. But he did make me run the Physical Fitness Test which, in those days was in "boots and utes" (utilities or BDUs as the Army calls them), a sure way to ruin your feet. Contemporary Marines still run the mandatory 3-miles in at least 29 minutes but do so in running shoes. Then, out of deference to the run difficulty in boots, the maximum allowed was 35 minutes. Common sense prevailed after the Vietnam War and the Corps changed the parameters of the PFT. Then the SOB made me stand the group's Commanding General's "uniform of the day" inspection which I flew through as soon as the inspecting officer saw my Vietnam campaign and combat actions ribbon. He flew right past me like I owned a Silver Star.

The final irony was that, on my last day of active duty, 13 September, he and the CO virtually begged me to apply to Officer Candidate School. But that meant, within a year, I'd be back in Southeast Asia, this time as a butter-bar 2nd Lieutenant.

In 1969, no thank you!

Then, just before permanently leaving the air station some "brother" Marine broke into my Volkswagon and stole a beautiful 35-mm Nikon camera I purchased in the Danang just before I left 'Nam. It was the final, tasteless insult before I flew out of the main gate minutes later. The guard at the gate stopped as my entry decal had expired and started giving me the requisite 'ration of shit' about how I needed to get a new one. Are you 'kiddin'me? A new decal on my last day of active duty?

I gave him the single-digit salute and drove off.

Right after I arrived at El Toro in the first week, one of the little sidebars of my time there, a couple of "spooks" from somebody's G-2 (intelligence section) in Washington, D. C. interviewed me in a recording booth at the El Toro headquarters building for more than three hours. Their questions honed over the infamous Jacques patrol down to the most minute detail I could remember for the historical record at Headquarters, Marine Corps. Much of the detail eludes me today but then it was violently and disturbingly fresh. Years later I read it in a proposed film documentary in Los Angeles and my own words were still very unnerving.

I had permission to leave active duty early under an order then in force that allowed Marines to exit early if they entered into a bachelor's degree program. In mid-July I submitted the appropriate paperwork through the Headquarters Group squadrons with the requisite signatures of release from the senior officer administrators of both the parent squadron and group. The package then went to 3rd MAW for final endorsement but sat listlessly in the office of the wing "career advisor" for almost six weeks.

No action.

So I went to this truly dumb-ass, single-digit IQ, then career adviser gunnery sergeant and asked why there was "no action" on the request for early release. This is his quoted reply.

"Well, sergeant, it doesn't say here specifically in the acceptance letter that the program(s) they offer at the University of California result in a bachelor's degree."

What we have here, to paraphrase and twist a quote from one of my favorite lines from the move "Hud," is ignorance wrapped around five stripes of a gunny. I was livid that he was that stupid. But he was.

"Gunny, it's the UNIVERSITY of California. That's all they offer, BAs, MAs, and PhDs."

This shall not pass so I left his office immediately, drove over to the registrar's office at UCI when the registrar actual, John Brown, took the copy of the Marine Corps Order and immediately drafted a new acceptance letter that even the most obtuse of Marines could understand. Brown was a class act and I am eternally grateful to both him and a stunning blonde student staffer (with whom I fell instantly in lust.) who made the immediate correction on the spot with the requisite letter. Without their timely reaction, I could not have started back to school in the fall of '68. But, by the time I returned to El Toro, the lame one previously noted had already "secured" for the afternoon. So I broke into his office via a window, put the letter into the package and on top of his ever so "heavy" in-basket so it would slap him in the face the next Monday.

By the following Friday the CG had signed the release.

One final last memory of my time at 3rd MAW was a harbinger of the ugly, contemporary future. At one time that summer I was summoned to the wing legal office to sign a non-disclosure to ANYONE regarding an ongoing investigation about an alleged drug ring that was smuggling marijuana from Old Mexico into the United States. I was tasked to do the administrative work. Allegedly both pilots and two members of the crew of a CH-46 were all part of the conspiracy to collect weed in Mexico and dump it for delivery in the California desert for pick-up. So CID (Criminal Investigation Department) assigned an investigator to infiltrate the unit. The investigator was a CID gunnery sergeant. I was told the helicopter crew in question left on a routine training mission with that same CID investigator. The next day the investigation was abruptly "secured," and they had no further need for me but the non-disclosure was active for life. I am now violating it. The case literally disappeared from view. Just before I left active duty, the investigator's body was purportedly found on the desert floor near El Centro, CA.

Ever hear about it since? Or did the CID gunny take the magic helicopter death leap? That was August of 1968.

Back forward to September, 1968 and now, consider this my confession. Patrick's entry into the UC system was technically fraudulent, deliberate and with premeditation as obviously I was and am NOT college material. Today the UC administration could "technically" yank the bachelor's degree (history/political science) from me that hangs just above my head at this desk. **"Oh, the horror!"** I fudged my way to get into the hallowed hall of Anteater learning (UCI) with that lapse of memory about Catholic U. But at 0600 this date (08 Feb 2016) the degree still hangs here "with all the rights and privileges thereunto pertaining" with four attesting signatures, the most prominent by then Board of Regents Gov. Ronald Reagan. I'm still looking for that lost coterie of rights and privileges. Millenials note. They're hard to find.

Post graduation, I went to Europe to join the blonde girlfriend who was there on a student-abroad program from Irvine and we dutifully trapesed around Europe with her younger brother through the museums of England, France, Austria, Italy via Eurail pass and even into the then East Germany (a very creepy experience). After six weeks of ignoring reality, return to the US came with a "thud." I had sold my new '68 Volkswagon to finance the trip so now it was the time to get....a job. After a plethora of said, I interviewed with Syntex Laboratories then most famous for a line of Norinyl birth-control pills and, thus, my first job was one of a legal drug salesman, promoting said with doctors and pharmacies in the Washington, D. C. area. The job rarely strayed from the mostly mundane except for one doctor named Sahakian near Beltsville, MD.

Syntex back then manufactured a cream for vaginitis called Vagitrol. It sold well and was very effective. When I would visit Dr. Shakian's office, he would take my entire trunk load of promotional Vagitrol I had for his patients, even though I noted that his patient load was balanced male to female. But, when I did "script checks" (illegal as hell but every good drug detailer does it), on what drugs he proscribed, I noted he wrote Vagitrol a ton......for me. Good for him and my sales quota. Then a pharmacist friend with whom I had unedited access to prescription histories, said: "Take a look at the names of patients." Ordinarily

I didn't care, just tallied the number of scripts written. It turns out he wrote Vagitrol for athlete's foot, a violation of protocol under the guidelines of the Physicians' Desk Reference (PDR). But here's the bottom line. It works and, if you can get over the ugly moss-green staining of your toes and feet, the fungus disappears.

I had another great physician who treated me for a minor case of hemorrhoids who proffered that the best way for junkies to ingest heroin was via suppository. No needle marks. Instant high! That tour of duty expanded my naiveté and experience in ways I could never imagine. After nine months on this civilian learning curve, I left Syntex and returned to California in June of '72. Actually I was "encouraged" to resign in lieu of firing because the sales district wasn't producing for a host of reasons, not all of which were my doing. I left Syntex sporting a full beard and no further job prospects, glad to return to the land of milk and honey........and a future bullet train. Then Disney called again. I worked there off and on for four years. This eventually became my final tour with the Mickey Mouse Club.

The first Mainstream Electrical Parade was about to go onto the street three days later in June'72 and the materials needed along with the assigned wardrobe crew were not ready for prime time. So Disney needed an experienced wardrobe hand to head the crew, violated their own ostensible contract with the prevailing service union and hired me back as the foreman. At first they initially offered "lead" pay of $1.98/hr. I re-buffed and laughed at it during the interview with Wardrobe Supervisor Don Hufstadler. But I didn't have enough money to go to lunch so I was the one bluffing. Disney recanted and offered full foreman pay at full-time for what I remember was about $3.60/hr. So at 26, I became the oldest member of the Wardrobe Parade Crew dressing and catering to dozens of coddled (predominantly female) adolescents oozing with all the attendant testosterone and estrogen energy. I jumped at the offer as hunger trumps everything and spent the next three months happily working among the panoply of dancers and performers hired for the parade from sundry high schools and colleges in the Orange County area. I had a crew of 8-12 permanent-part time wardrobe attendants (affectionately known as "rag pickers") within a highly sex-charged environment that created a host of memorable leadership problems.

It always astounded me the number of young women in that 1968-1972 era age group, and maybe now, who did not/do not know their own bra size. That's not a sexist comment, just an empirical observation relevant to the Disney age group of that summer. Maybe women today are collectively more enlightened and aware. I hope so. Every shift, consequently, found one or two performers on average who would show up for work, sometimes directly from the beach, braless and in a minor panic. Disney dress regulation forbids the display of nipples in Disney costumes. After all, this is "family" entertainment. We had spare bras in stock for those said afflicted with wardrobe memory lapse but the conversation between the wardrobe attendants and the "braless babes" were truly priceless. They were always amazed that we could guess the approximate breast size of the volume and width of the human female.

"Say, you look like a 36B! Trust me! I'm a professional at this." The return looks were truly...........priceless!

The entire panoply of the Disneyland costumes depended on assessing the appropriate size of a woman's anatomy before issue of a costume for a particular attraction. A size 8 in a Fantasyland costume, for instance, might require a 12 in Tomorrowland. Disney, however, also had a full-time wardrobe consultant (un-affectionately known as the "wardrobe bitch" by employees in the park and on the parade) who trolled through the park to find women who spotted obsequious costume violations that included too much eye make-up, no bra or minor infractions like "rolling the waistline" of their skirts to hike the hemline in Small World. Males had no such hazard, provided they kept their hair at the appropriate short length. If the violation was egregious enough, Disney would take the employee off shift and sent them home without pay. So the "Whiskey Bravo" garnered no love from the females among the Disney performers. Since we dressed some of them from the pantyhose or tights outward, the initial two parades were an exercise in controlled chaos. Marines would call it a Charley-Foxtrot or a "cluster-fuck." We dressed the performers for their particular dance segment as they moved down Mainstreet Disneyland but the regalia were often illegal and entirely too heavy for the dancers to wear. State labor codes then strictly mandated that women weighing less than 120 pounds could not perform carrying these awkward, unbalanced loads that sometimes weighed up to 50 pounds. Very early it came to critical. It was load versus percentage of your body weight.

One young high school dancer who weighed about 90 lbs from Loara High School in Anaheim literally passed out during one of the first parades in June that year. Disney had two parades at dusk and 9:00 at night, each going in the opposite direction. She passed out on Mainstreet with her lighted "flower" during the second parade of the night with a wet cell battery on her hip that also weighed about 3-5 pounds. Combine that with the weight of the harness and "flower" she carried in the dance routine, she collapsed from a combination of weight and dehydration. We quickly hustled her off to the nurse's aid station on a stretcher in front of the adoring parade crowd. But they were aghast. She suffered no permanent injury but the electrical flower lay dead on the street until we came back to retrieve it for the parades the next day.

The next more memorable event came on one of the ensuing Sundays.

One of the floats in the first parade was this awkward Elizabethan-era group with dancers in huge hoop skirts mimicking the dress of that time with six male dancers carrying a large canopy above them. I had previously warned the costume and wardrobe department managers via memo that the wet cell batteries were hazardous and regularly leaked with a recommendation that we use dry cells to light the myriad lights on the costumes themselves that the dancers wore. "Budget" constraints carried the day and suggestion ignored.

Sundays were always the day that the parade had virtually no supervision because most supervisors opted to take off work on weekends.

I then became the senior Disney employee on site.

Just before the step-off of the parade one Sunday, one of the dance performers said "My back is burning," and began to panic. Another member of the male crew and I then went to her aid, and ripped off the very heavy hoop skirt with a thick canvas waist belt off her. The battery acid had leaked into her perianal area and pudendum so I shredded her pantyhose, put her on a bench, wiped the offensive acid from her vaginal area and immediately applied ice to her buttock and groin. The burning subsided and we wrapped her in several towels and called for a nurse at the nurses' station to come back into the staging area as I was not about to take a semi-naked woman through the park itself. The nurse applied salve to the area and she suffered no further skin damage except the embarrassment of nude exposure to her peers in the dance troupe. Her name, and I remember it quite distinctly: Caprice Blaze! I believe she took a couple of days off work but, upon return, planted a "Thank you!" kiss on me for prevention of what could have been an emergency room experience.

Disneyland's response: A formal written reprimand for me by exposing her buttock and genitalia. The letter further scolded me for my action by not waiting for the nurse to arrive and apply the required first-aid. Also note that the nurses' station was more than 500 yards away from the back staging area of the parade. No suspension, just a "don't be a bad boy again" letter and never do it again! Caprice's kiss made up for the corporate stupidity of the reprimand.

At the end of the "parade" season I transferred back to the day shift in the main wardrobe with the "older" crew of attendants, many of whom had been there since 1955 when the park opened. The gig was easy as most of these attendants could do the assigned tasks by rote memory and never gave the foreman a bad time. They were all on the quiet road to a Disney retirement. I kept track of break and lunch times for crew members in my head but suffered from a daily case of abject boredom that led to my final resignation by Christmas of '72 to return to return to Irvine for the teacher credentialing program. That was a return to peripheral poverty but I finished the credential program in fewer than six months. And it was on to teaching as an adolescent animal trainer.

The Gulf War
Conversations About the
Hangover of Easy Victory

In the spring of 1987 doubts about whether I should remain a second-ary teacher led me on a spiritual journey back to the Marine Corps, 13 more years of service and eventual deployment in the Gulf War.

It was an inspired, circuitous route.

At the time I was teaching math at Wilmington Junior High School (part of the Los Angeles Unified District), fewer than six blocks from the house where my wife grew up in the "harbor area" of Los Angeles that annexed Wilmington and its neighbor city of San Pedro in 1906. Outside of California, relatively few Americans know that LA proper is more than 20 miles north of its own harbor and annexed a 16-mile strip from the city proper on both sides of the Harbor Freeway that leads directly to the port. In effect, they stole the harbor. By the end of World War II the independent commission that now runs the mon-strous port employed more than 90,000 and remains today the central hub for goods and cargo from a plethora of Asian countries along the rim of Asia along with the port of Long Beach in Southern California.

I had just married Anita at her home parish in Wilmington and I decided to take five days of sick leave and privately re-assess my direction in life at the Prince of Peace Benedictine Abbey in San Clemente, CA directly adjacent and abutting Camp Pendleton. At the time, I was 42 years old. The abbey is a marvelous place for a solitary or marital meditation that I highly recommend to anyone seeking to retreat and re-examine their lives away from the scourge and panoply of noise that afflicts modern life everywhere. Then the monks asked for a simple $20/day stipend for lodging, provided three meals per day that are simple, elegant and filling, access to the Benedictine priests who live there for counseling and the solitude of one of the most magnificent chapels in all of California with a stunning wooden mural of Christ in back of the altar. The mural is the artistic product of a monk who then was at another of the Benedictine abbeys in old Mexico. If you're reading this thus far, go to the internet and query Prince of Peace Abbey in San Clemente and savor the quiet it delivers.

On day four of this spiritual sojourn, I was walking on the ridge north of the abbey proper toward Pendleton base housing when I observed a lengthy arc of CH-46 helicopters elevating from somewhere near "mainside" onto one of the Navy's helicopter- attack carriers like the USS Tarawa or Peleliu. They were about 15-miles away so there was no noise to obstruct or interfere with the visual of the movement.

Dead silence with a question: What in my life both fulfilled and elevated me to the human being I try to be today? Two answers: The education endowed by the Marist Fathers of the Society of Mary (And, yes, they are Catholic!) and the U. S. Marine Corps. I suddenly became very clear as I felt God was whispering a very clear message, urging me to heed. I felt like I just gotten a Jethro Gibbs head slap. And for those of you pandering agnostics and atheists filled with yourself about his non-existence, take a hike and live with your vacuous assumptions and the void in your heart. We'll tally the votes in the afterlife.

When I returned home the following Friday at roughly 1600, I called the then Marine Corps Reserve recruiter in Los Angeles near Chavez Ravine where the LA Dodgers play. What follows is a para-phrased transcript of that cryptic conversation:

"Good afternoon, Marine, would you be interested in recruiting an old Marine with a master's degree and combat experience? Thus ensued the traditional, perfunctory silence every Marine recognizes. Then the reply:

"Wait one!"

Every Marine or sailor who ever made that phone call on active duty has heard that reply incessantly. Translation: "I really don't know what the fuck to do with this conversation so I'll seek 'guidance' from higher authority who may know what the hell to do next." Three days later (Monday next), the recruiter called back and already had a faxed copy of my service record in hand.

"The Corps is prepared to bring you back as a corporal, sir!"
My reply was curt and flippant. "I left the jungle in Vietnam and El Toro as a sergeant. I'm coming back as a sergeant."

The conversation abruptly ended and I was somewhat despondent at the lame reply but, two days later, the recruiter called again and said a new unit called the 3ʳᵈ Civil Affairs Unit was interested in me and, yes, Kansas City (the central records depository) said I could return as a sergeant. So the newly re-minted Sergeant Patrick J. Fitch reported that Friday for the requisite swearing-in and the mound of paperwork that accompanies a re-enlistment, including the perfunctory physical. At that point I had 19 years "broken time" in service parlance. Exit in 1968; re-entry in 1987. I arrived after school hours at Chavez ravine prepared to do all the above. To my surprise, I found myself on my first active drill weekend active in civilian clothes for a Command Post Exercise that mimicked what the unit would do in actual combat. That began my regular reserve commitment that lasted another 13 years until Dec. 7, 2000. I then met LtCol Larry Gonzalez, a principal in the same system I taught, and thought I was there for an interview after the I&I (Instructor and Inspection staff: Active duty overseers of reserve units) sent me to him. The interview was curt and immediate. He led me to tent, showed me to a radio set and intoned………

"Do you remember how to use one of these?"

Welcome back to the Marine Corps. The interview became an active duty drill……… with applied points to any future Federal pension. It was one of the best feelings in all my adult life. Grab a weapon, jump onboard and savor the upcoming patrol. God, it was good to be back! Those of you who know not the fraternity that is the U. S. Marine Corps may not understand. It is both a spiritual commitment to God, country and fraternity. They were and we are among the finest contingent of human beings committed to America's survival as a nation. We gunslingers of all service branches, are the true One Percent. And take no shit from the boorish subset of aggrieved whiners who adore Uncle Bernie in 2016.

I was "jacked up" to be back! Then came Saddam Hussein.

In August of 1990 the Sergeant Major of the 3rd CAG called me on behalf of the command and asked me to volunteer for the "advance party" from 3rd CAG forming to go to Saudi Arabia in anticipation of the coming war with Iraq in August of 1990. Since Anita was eight months pregnant, I declined. "I didn't volunteer for the first war and will not volunteer for this."

"I'll gladly go……just show me the orders." As a side note, every set of orders that came during my 13 years in the Marine Corps reserve, the Corps only trusted FedEx, not the United States Postal Service. Take that for what it's worth. Maybe there was some obscure Federal mandate to do that but I suspect it spoke more to the trust of the then USPS. My reluctance to "volunteer" stems from the harsh reality of my previous combat at Khe Sanh and the fact that my daughter, Adriana, was due to arrive in late September. Our obstetrician said she would arrive approximately 10 October. I demurred and predicted she would arrive earlier than his 40-week standard calendar that doctors predict from the end of the last menstrual cycle. I counted the exact days from conception, 21 December 1989, and knew exactly the day she was conceived.

I was there for the party.

She arrived on time, straight vaginal birth in the early AM of September 21st, the same day as my father's birthday. So much for the precision of medical calculations! To distort one of my mother's favorite bromides: Doctors propose; babies dispose. Infants follow a different schedule.

The orders arrived in early December and the 3rd CAG rallied at Camp Pendleton and trained for three weeks in preparation for embarkation and finally gathered with family there at Pendleton for a final good-bye before transit to then Norton Air Force base in San Bernadino. The scene quietly turned somber and teary-eyed. Note the picture taken of me grabbing Anita's hand on the front cover at which I contemplated might be the last time we ever saw one another. It was and still is emotionally gut-wrenching. I was one of the few Marines in the unit who had actually seen real combat, a host of dead Marine bodies, and scores of wounded. The 3rd CAG's CO then was John Kaheny with whom I served during the '68 Tet Offensive with the 26th Marines at Khe Sanh and can he tell you true stories of literally "sleeping with the dead" during the Hill Fights of 881 and 861 north of Khe Sanh because the incoming was too heavy to evacuate the dead bodies. At that point, only John and I and then gunnery sergeant Sam Cicchino were the only members of the 121-member unit who had tasted the "slimey" aftertaste of what we might expect.

We aren't the Boy Scouts of America and Kuwait was not Valley Forge, PA. I knew exactly what we might confront in Iraq and it was sobering. The flight via Germany to Saudi Arabia took the better part of four full-length feature films almost 18 hours aboard a commercial airliner that was about as quiet in transit as a Trappist monastery. No animated fake, bravado or loud braggadocio. The quarters were cramped with our seabags, our rifles or pistols and our reflective thoughts.

And contemplate this. Each of us also had an issue of 120 rounds of M-16 ammunition so we were ready to come off the plan in Saudi ready for any contingency and had enough killing power to decimate a small Latin American dictatorship. This isn't a "sea story" and that "ain't no shit"!

The first leg of the trip stopped in then West Germany where we exited the cramped quarters of the aircraft and several of my peers made what they considered an amazing, enlightened discovery, automated vending machines for beer.

Dorothy, you're not in Utah anymore!

I don't remember if we were under orders not to drink but no one did as we were in the mood for it. Then Murphy appeared at the end of the flight. We arrived late at night and it was another "Charley Foxtrot" as so many planes were transporting troops that the tarmac had its quota of guests. Welcome to Saudi! Now mill around and pretend to know what the fuck you're doing. After several days of housing in

GP (general purpose) tents whose design dates back to World War II, the unit shifted to these barracks structures that the Saudis used to house their guests workers from other countries. True to form, they segregated the help by nationality. Thus Bengladeshis could not cohabit with Phillipinos etc, etc. All fresh water came in bottles and the food in the mess halls, provided by the Saudis, was barely edible with obviously any selections of pork. Here, in the South, it is high treason that warrants the death penalty. I prefer both C-rations and MRE's to the cheap cuisine they served. They spent little of that precious oil money on the Infidels saving their royal asses from the Big Bad Saddam.

Then I was part of a contingent sent aboard the Persian Gulf fleet that floated around near Kuwait City on the fake landing force that was really a diversion for the brilliant end-around maneuver that made our whole war excursion almost moot. We even went so far as to do a fake landing drill in Oman where we boarded a World War II "Higgins" landing craft (yes, the same ones used at the landing at Normandy) and arrived at the beach soaking wet, only to be dry within 20 minutes.

Desert heat has that effect.

Back onboard ship, we were still under the illusion that we really were "going to hit the beach." Several days later we attended a briefing where the Master Sergeant briefer from the Marine Expeditionary Force yanked my sorry, sleeping ass to attention with: "3rd CAG, we're moving you up from the 7th wave up to the 3rd wave." No one in our CAG contingent reacted. My hand then shot up.

"Top, 3rd Civil Affairs Group, why are we in the 3rd wave?"

An unnamed officer with our group, who will remain nameless to protect his innocence, asked me: "Sergeant Fitch, don't you want to be upfront and wet?" My response was deliberately sarcastic and fringe flippant. "Are you out of your fucking mind......Sir? Upfront, wet and dead and we never get to perform our mission. That makes me sad"

Just to confirm it. Many of my heroes from my two wars are very dead. I had no desire at 45 to join them. The net result of our 3-week float was that it worked tactically but our shipboard contingent then was summarily ordered back to dry land where we joined a convoy near the port city of Al Jubail, then shot west toward the desert breech point, stopped at an ad hoc fuel dump and started through the one-lane strip that the combat engineers created with explosive charges and this nifty anti-tank mine machine with a tank base and extended teeth that dug up and sometimes detonated any enemy mines. The convoy then stopped momentarily in the cleared breech point and, suddenly explosive-like flashes erupted all up and down the convoy.

Memories of mortars stoked my adrenaline and I leaped from our Hummvee, and rolled away from the vehicle. Laughter rained on my ass from my fellow "Cagsters" in the hummer as the "flashings" were all from Marines with cameras taking souvenir pictures like they were at Desert Disneyland. As the convoy moved forward, we hit the "hard-ball" asphalt road toward Kuwait City, rushed forward at 55mph, then suddenly stopped. I suggested to Captain Alphonse Faison ("Leather-head" as we affectionately knew him) that we exit the vehicle in case this stop was unplanned and I was thinking ambush. Nothing happened but my sense of dread was not assuaged. Then the colonel in charge of this convoy of dogs and cats sped it around in the opposite direction. Twenty-minutes later he stopped the convoy a second time and turned it around to proceed north again. That prompted my next editorial comment among to sleepy Marines in the hummer.

"I believe this son-of-a-bitch is lost! We're in deep shit."

No one else in the hummer either responded or seemed concerned. I felt like the scapegoat, taking on everyone's secret fear and enunciating it publicly. Unlike my peers, only "Termite," the driver and I were completely alert. Fatigue ruled the night and I very distinctly remembered how fatigue was as deadly a weapon as a malfunctioning rifle in Vietnam. I really wanted dawn to break and it did just as we arrived at the Kuwait International Airport.

This was now Day 3 of the war. We exited the vehicle and, out of nowhere came the Marine Corp's most dangerous, inert weapon: A gunnery sergeant with a clipboard who needed a 'detail' to help mark unexploded ordnance scattered all over the airport runways.

"November, Foxtrot, Whiskey," I shouted at him. "We're a civil affairs unit, not trained to do that assignment."

"Well, I'm the senior gunnery sergeant here, sergeant! And I'm ordering you and your men to join this detail."

"Well, that' not going to happen, gunny," although the response was a bit more colorful. I immediately went to get our lieutenant colonel in command of our contingent. The colonel amended the gunnery sergeant's order and attitude. That's how it works. The big dog slaps the underdog, the Alpha male prevails and life goes forward.

Suddenly it's Day 4. The war ends and we return to the most sober barracks in Marine Corps history in Al Jubail, Saudi Arabia. Remember the Marine Corps' founders were a bunch or roiling, fighting drunkards in a tavern in Philadelphia. Never forget that. But we acceded to the wishes of our hosts. Now it's 2016 and the Saudis desperately need both our assistance with personnel and material to fend off their Shiite nemeses. Sobriety not needed here, just a bunch of street fighters willing to kill on their behalf. This may not be in our country's best interest but I'd give them the "Welcome to New York speech!" And tell them we'll help......as soon as their multitudes of young Sunni men enlist to save the Saudi Royal Family from extinction.

Then, and only then, should we risk more American blood. Unless they can devise a way to eat oil or turn it into tofu, we'll stick with the fracked American variant.

Within the week after the cessation of hostilities, we were offered the chance to assess the damage done on the "Highway of Death." It was a strange trip. Unlike my Cagster cohorts, I was very familiar with decaying bodies. That and "nuoc mam" from Vietnam, the condiment of choice for Vietnamese, are permanently embedded in my brain housing group.

We then took this "after-action" field trip to the site of the infamous "Highway of Death" where United States pilots caught the retreating Iraqis on the main highway from Kuwait to Bagdad. The smell and the visuals were bad. One of my sustaining memories was of a group of British nurses literally "posing" in a jeep-like Soviet vehicle next to a dead Iraqi driver.

His face was half blown off so he went to the afterlife with a classic case of Priapism with the nurses relishing what might have been with someone that well-endowed in real life. They had a great time with the corpse but I doubt the multitude of pictures they took will make it to their Gulf War cruise book for their grandchildren.

Yes, war is strange.

Ejection from a Catholic Mass to Meeting My Wife, Anita

Truth always gestates a better story than most fiction but what happened in July 1985 began a series of events that pre-cursed my marriage the ensuing year.

I was living at the time in a small house I bought near 20th St. between Long Beach Bouevard and Pacific Avenue in Long Beach, CA when I decided to go to Sunday mass at Holy Innocents Catholic parish that was within walking distance of my home. Remember, I was what then was called a "lapsed Catholic." It was an abysmally hot day for the beach city and the temperature hovered near 95F, a rarity that close to the ocean. The church, moreover, had no air-conditioning system, just ceiling high casement windows fully opened to allow some semblance of ventilation. Appropriate to the weather, I wore pleated walking shorts (not cut-offs fancied by so many beach visitors), a polo, collared shirt and long socks with clean running shoes.

But that ensemble was entirely inappropriate for one of the battalion of Filipino ushers at Holy Innocents, who patrolled and policed the aisles parish church with solemn verve in their best suits and ties. The priest entered and the Mass was about to begin. It was Pentecost season on the Catholic calendar so the mass celebrant priest wore green vestments in an environment with which I was totally familiar. An usher then approached me at the north end of the center pews, excoriated me for my "inappropriate dress" and ordered me to leave the church.

Yet, here I was, a cradle Catholic, summarily ejected from a Catholic church from an usher acting more like a major league umpire thumbing out a miscreant ballplayer. I failed the dress code! "Oh, the horror!," as Colonel Kurtz said in "ApocalyseNow," cited earlier. I couldn't possibly go to heaven or talk to Jesus unless I changed into more formal attire. Not willing to create a scene, I opted for retreat but, before I left, I noticed a brochure in the vestibule of the church for a Catholic "Choice Weekend" for singles 39 and under.

I was riding the rim of eligibility for said as I was 40.

At the time I was dating some "interesting" women with a boxcar load of baggage somewhere between sexually exotic and "in dire need of Gestalt therapy." You know the stereotype: Two ex-husbands or "ex-somethings" with kids in three different zip codes. Dating for recreation use has its place and I was fond of it but didn't want a "rescue romance" with the attendant trauma that goes with the package. So I admit I was "Looking for Love in all the Wrong Places" and, as Hank Williams Jr. croons, I almost always opted for "Naked Women and Beer." Along with my fellow Vietnam alumni, I was quite fond of naked women since I returned from Quang Tri Province, South Vietnam in 1968, gave up beer some years later but tired of the role of Mr. Fix-it for many of the women I met. A lothario I was; I shrink I was not.

This is thus my confession. I was as profligate as St. Augustine and I knew it was time to modify my approach as I wanted a family and, as much as I admit the difficult role of step-father, I wanted my kids to share my DNA.

I'll, therefore, confess to the venial sin of selfishly wanting to have my own children. Ok? Get over it!

After some badgering from the two women on the brochure/flyer who honchoed the program, I opted for the November weekend at a retreat house in Dominguez Hills, CA. The "Choice Program" was a brilliant inception sponsored by the Archdiocese of Los Angeles that included a young, very-hip priest and two married couples who led us in seminars about the gritty elements of a cohesive marriage: Sex, money, in-laws, religious values and a variety of uncomfortable topics that most single people either don't address or know how until the big "D" word comes up in later years. There were roughly 30 singles on my retreat weekend and it was a real revelation.

Almost all the women in the group of retreatants were Hispanic (Welcome to CA!), college educated and drop-dead- attractive, articulate, funny and a joy to be around. Yes, I was looking for love in the wrong places and this was a new phase......and the right place. As Anita tells it, she went to the retreat in July with a woman who became a dear friend of hers, later sang at our wedding and noticed me at the closing mass on Sunday because none of the other retreatants on my weekend wanted to talk about what they learned or found inspiring in those 2.5 days in November. I have no problem with public speaking so I was the first to jump up and run my mouth. I do that often.

It's an Irish thing!

The older married couple from the November retreat afterwards arranged a Christmas Party for all of us from both the July and November retreats at their condo/apartment complex in Torrance, CA. There I first noticed Anita. And yes, like Jimmy Carter, I had lust in my heart. What the hell, lust was my favorite capital sin. I pursued it with vigor and thought I was being slick, talking to everyone, moving around the room when I noticed her moving around the pool table in the complex. I went into hormonal overdose seeing this size 4 woman who then weighed 108. Today most women her peers would kill to be as healthy and attractive. At 60 she's a size 7 and still qualifies as "energetically warm." She said she saw me coming, she knew what I wanted (and it wasn't heretofore mentioned Baked Alaska). We exchanged phone numbers. Here comes some divine intervention.

Anita was living next door to her parents in Wilmington, CA in a small house that they owned. She had no phone. When I called her the next day, her brother, Richard, answered and said he'd get her. Then I heard this loud cow bell summoning her from the adjacent rental house of her parents.

I was within seconds of hanging up as my first thought was: "This chick is too weird! What the hell is that all about?" When she finally arrived for the call, we arranged our first date and then an ensuing one in which we walked the beach in Belmont Shore for almost four hours where we had one of the most intense, honest, sexually-charged, mature conversation of both our adult lives. We deeply kissed at the end of that afternoon, and probably both knew at that point, although reluctant to say it. We were going to marry. After two more almost daily intense weeks of dating, we were back at my house in Long Beach watching Dick Clark ring in 1986. At midnight we almost beat each other to the punch with the inevitable question and became engaged. May 24 later we married. Despite reservations from my own sister and a number of my other friends that we seemed too dissimilar for such a union to last amid a multitude of reasons why, we will celebrate our 30th wedding anniversary this May 24, 2016. So much for outside wisdom and interference! Flag on the play!

Ya'll were wrong.

On wedding day I claimed that cow bell from my mother-in-law.

It is now attached to the wall outside the north door to our house here in Kentucky where we can alert Anita to come inside for dinner from her studio.

I'd like to be buried with it. It peals the seal of the marriage. Symbols are important and, every time I ring it, it lightens my evening.

License to Master's

January '72 began my long tenure and foray into secondary teaching that began with licensing/credential work that varies slightly from state to state. The trek to license included such titillating courses as "History of Education," "Methods of Teaching Elementary Art" and the ever so popular, required "Psychological Foundations of Education." All these courses were sonorous but mandatory. The California programs had parallel strands, one elementary (K-6) and another secondary (7-12). I initially opted to do both but saw the light very early that I wanted to teach older students with the attendant opportunity to coach afterschool sports.

The historic tally of hours toward any degree meant that a semester course of three hours the class met for three hours per week every semester of roughly 24 weeks. So over a period of four years, you would take 40 courses or independent studies, totaling 120 semester hours toward whatever your degree is. The quarter system like UC (Irvine) had/has allocates four "quarter" units per class for full-time enrollment so a quarter system would theoretically require passage of 48 courses over the same four-year time frame or slightly more than 190 "quarter" units. Twelve quarter units, or four classes, per 10-week session was/is a full load. With the quarter system, as soon as you start, rest assured that the mid-term examinations or research papers were less a month away. No time for lollygagging and easing into the volume of work. The ambush always came when a student transferred from a school on the semester system to the quarter one and what your new "academic mother ship" would accept from your old school and the pace of a 10-week cycle required. I decided to accelerate the credential process that included student teaching at both the elementary and secondary levels in six months (January to August) so I could be employed by September.

That was the "plan."

Like most plans, they instantly modify when the first incoming round comes downrange. Since I worked 30-40 hours per week during my undergraduate years, I didn't mingle with the social crowd on the faculty and only closely knew J. Alan Rogers, now Professor Emeritus at Boston College who mentored my senior thesis on the Western Pennsylvania Whiskey Rebellion of 1794 at Irvine.

Alan wrote a marvelous letter supporting my admission to the Department of Education that was quite legitimate but the other two required letters came from two long-term friends of mine in college administration. Those two were articulate pieces of remarkable, academic fiction, about as true as Grimm's Fairy Tales but they got the job done. Admission secured, the program started in January.

Attempting to jump-start the process, I enrolled in 20 quarter hours in the winter and received the perfunctory letter of admonition that I needed to drop down to 16 hours per quarter as the addition of a fifth class would imperil my academic standing progress. The letter ordered me to drop one of the five classes so I did the rationale thing: I ignored it. Yeah, like a directed reading class in history might damn me to academic hell. But I knew the nuances of the off-site computer enrollment system then housed at UCLA with all the Irvine academic records that only caught "over-enrollment" weeks after the fact.

The trick then was Irvine used UCLA to track student schedules so I enrolled for 16 units in mid-December and, a week later, 16 more for a total of 32. Thus, when I dropped back to 20 quarter hours, disenrolled in 12 as per the admonition, the computer and the administration left me alone. Ten weeks later, 20 units of "A" completed, came the spring quarter. Uno mas! I did the same thing again. Arriving at the summer session, I had whacked out most of the perfunctory and desultory course work except one in "Secondary School Curriculum." When I went to the department secretary and told her that I was going to take an "incomplete" (I) grade and finish it in the summer, she assumed the schoolmarm stance:

"Dr. Bailey doesn't allow incompletes"

"Well, I'm a 27-year-old combat Marine vet, and I will take the incomplete." I was too irritated with the canned response and withdrew from any confrontation, opting instead to deal with it later.

I was, however, spared that academic fistfight as Dr. Ken Bailey gave me my only "C" and essentially four free units for a class I never attended nor for which I did any work. "Muchas gratias" for the "freebie." Just another hoop out of the way! The net result was that, by August, I had the secondary credential, dropped two courses for the elementary one and left Irvine with a 3.8 graduate GPA and a secondary credential. Years later that GPA course load, about as difficult to pass as day's worth of prized urine, became the rationale upon which the University of Arizona cited and awarded me a graduate fellowship in journalism in 1979.

In '79 I was teaching two journalism classes at San Gabriel (CA) High School with a small coterie of very, very bright teens, all of whom were immensely talented and personable. It was the most fun year I ever had in teaching as I watched with profound amazement how they just took the award-winning school newspaper and ran it like professionals. I was a paid spectator at in my own classroom. But they politely informed me that it was "their" newspaper and do the adult thing by behaving as I was told by the student staff. They taught me as much about ambition, organization and commitment to an enterprise as any similar group of adults I ever met. Wish I could see them all again today.

During the fall semester, I kept getting a series of phone calls from the Chicano Media Arts Association of Los Angeles about a weekend forum they planned to host at the Plaza del Raza in East Angeles in January of '79 where they would invite Mexican-American and Spanish-speaking kids to pitch the idea of the college pursuit of a journalism career. The Association is was, and likely still is, the crème de la crème of minority LA Hispanics in the media media market that included luminaries like Linda Alvarez, Marge Velasquez, Mario Machado and a host of others whose names now elude me. It was a very classy weekend replete with entertainment and excellent Mexican food but my staff on the "San Gabriel Matador" was pre-dominantly Asian and Caucasian....you know: That group that comedian George Carlin once called a shoe style. Undeterred, the calls continued, pleading for more Latin students to attend. Since I had none on staff, I went myself and that's when I met two of the faculty from the UA J-School who strongly encouraged me to apply to their graduate program in journalism. So I spent the $25 and submitted the application the next week and promptly forgot about it.

Much to my literal surprise, I then got a letter of acceptance that April along with the award of a graduate "fellowship" that covered the first year of the two-year program as free. So I called the registrar's office and asked why I was awarded the fellowship.

"Well, Mr. Fitch, of all the graduate applications this year, you had the highest GPA of any of the out-of-state candidates and the department awarded you one of two "out-of-state" graduate fellowships for this academic year."

"No shit!"

So I sold my house in Long Beach, moved to Tucson, and immediately bought another one.

Why?

Under Arizona law, the moment you purchase your primary residence in the state, you become an instant Arizona resident. That meant I paid tuition at the in-state resident rate for the second year of the program.

Net result: the total pay-out for my two-year master's degree program was $321.

Try finding one of those bargains today.

Assault on the 5th
Suzette Kelo v. the City of New London (2005)

Without much fanfare the U. S. Supreme Court rendered a decision in 2005 that shredded, then effectively excised the last clause of the 5th Amendment, commonly called the "takings clause," and thus permanently expanded the scope and reach of "eminent domain." That is the legal phrase that requires just compensation accorded private individuals and entities when public agencies seize their private property for "public use." The subtle distinction here is the majority changed the intent of the concept of "public use" to "public purpose." It was, in fact, a selection of words from "use" to "purpose" that now distorts the original meaning of the amendment. What the public uses from schools to parks is clearly evident to any reasonable man. The city of New London twisted that to mean "purpose" that would justify their creation of a new economic zone under which the city could levy new taxes on businesses therein that would accord New London enhanced revenue.

The 5th Amendment clearly peals the alarm with "No person shall......nor....be deprived of life, liberty or property." Carefully note the last phrase of the amendment.

Only those members of the American brain-dead public do not know of their "Miranda" rights as enunciated in the famed 1961 Miranda v. Arizona case that had been the lynchpin of hundreds of media courtroom dramas. But self- incrimination is not the only thing the vaunted 5th forbids. It also prohibits "double jeopardy" prosecution for the same crime (ala O. J. Simpson!), illegal custodial interrogation to coerce confessions, the right to refuse to testify against oneself along with the right to prosecutorial "due process."

Often overlooked, however, is that final "takings clause" because the obvious intent of the Constitution's framers was to allow public agencies the right of eminent domain to acquire property for public use only. Such public uses, for example, would include sites for a post office, a public transit system, a fire station, a park, a school or any other purpose to support access for and by the general public. What the Supremes did (with a 5-4) decision was to set a precedent where a public agency, the City of New London, CN, took the "private property/residence" of Suzette Kelo and gave it to another private entity, a private developer, to create business structures that would allegedly bring more than 3,000 jobs to the city. New London hoped to enhance the city's property tax base with inflated tax revenues from the new structures on the site. That's a legitimate goal for the city but here's the irony!

Although the city agreed to move Ms. Kelo's family home to a new location and pay substantial compensation to her and other homeowners, the plan collapsed in failure. The developer was eventually unable to obtain financing for the project and abandoned it. Thus the city was left with an empty lot, an aggrieved public and angry defendants forced to move against their will.

The land over which this legal infamy occurred is now a city dump. Welcome to stupidity at the municipal level.

But the court via *"stare decisis"* (Latin: to stand by [prior] decisions) then set a new precedent for citation/excuse by governments entities to take other property with similar intent. Those jurisdictions will rue the day the Court rendered this decision by the simple change of the words "use" to "purpose." What now constitutes use was mangled and muddled by the Supremes. Just what defines purpose? Justice John Paul Stevens delivered the death knell to Ms. Kelo with the majority opinion.

"Promoting economic development is a tradition and long accepted function of government," he said. "Clearly, there is no basis for exempting economic development from our traditionally broad understanding of public purpose."

Judicial activism once again trumped the Bill of Rights. And common sense somehow found new law encoded within the confines of the 5th.............with just one, little, seven-letter word. Use deferred; purpose preferred.

What the Court did was open a new can of worms, to browbeat an old cliché, that will pre-curse the process by which municipal, county and state agencies can invade your home and evict you under the pretense of some higher "purpose." And that becomes whatever the condemnation entity says it is.

James Madison might have a problem with that. I know I do, as do several million other Americans. The precedent decision is disturbing on multiple levels.   When a mere nine with a 5-4 eternal split can effectively parse and shred sections of the Constitution, what does that augur? And Donald Trump touts that as progress?

Please!

I submit to the jury that it is a loss of liberty never to be recovered. Revere not the change and modification of meaning. It has caustic implications. Forget the bombast of the "Trumpster" now in 2016 who never met an eminent domain he didn't like. The chilling effects of the frayed opinion of five judges effectively rendered a large chunk of American liberty null and void.

Post Scriptum

When I first arrived in what was then the Republic of (South) Vietnam, I sincerely believed that the good intentions of the Cold War prevailed and we should assist the South Vietnamese resist the de facto Marxist dictatorship of the north. That illusion dissipated almost instantly upon arrival in country and my commitment to defend was not for the mirage of democracy in the south but for the lives and honor of the Marines with whom I served. We Cold Warriors, now euphemistically part of the Baby Boomer generation, witnessed the lamest commitment to victory and subsequent retreat in U. S. history by 1975. It should not have happened.......but it did. So where are we?

The recent exposure of butchery and murder of more than 2,000 Vietnamese by their Viet Cong/NVA conquerors near Hue City is just a sad reminder of the unintended consequence of a half-hearted approach to combat and depletion of moral fortitude. I stepped into the breach as part of that One Percent of patriotic warriors and would argue the following. Not stepping into the fray of combat with anything less than a full commitment forebodes, in fact, a precursor of surrender and the ascension of evil. If democracies cede to centuries of tribal and ethnic resentments and vengeance dating back before the time of

Christ, it's game over. So, if the USA responds to a genuine threat from outside the United States, it needs to utterly, completely neutralize and destroy that threat first.

Then talk peace.

Send that message to both the Cognac-swilling little fat Korean prick with nukes in his arsenal and the death cult of ISIS. If the country avoids the hard choice to destroy them, the future of the West is bleak

When I first had the idea of this book, where I thought it would end was not what I planned at inception. It is very much like my senior history thesis on the Western PA Whiskey Rebellion of 1794 where I arrived at conclusions not warranted by from the premise of the start. So I hope this peripatetic traverse from youth to senior reflects a parallel course also taken by many of my peers. Much like what is reflected in the history of film, I'll stretch here for a metaphor.

We went from "Apocalyse Now" through "Coming Home," "Blackhawk Down" to "Lone Survivor," each within two generations with a kernel, a piece of wisdom in each. After the recent beheadings and systemic rapes by Islamic-Fascists in both the Middle East, Western Europe and here, the world is almost somnolent. What an indictment of moral corruption and indifference.

So heed my final homily: "Si vis pacem, para Bellum!" The strong survive. The weak are the prey.

CPSIA information can be obtained
at www.ICGtesting.com
Printed in the USA
LVOW08s0050091116
512214LV00022BA/229/P